FREEBIES
for
CAT
LOVERS

FREEBIES for CAT LOVERS

Produced by Bruce Nash and Allan Zullo

Compiled by Maria E. Grau Dieckmann and Ginger Kuh

Illustrated by Mack McKenzie

Prince Paperbacks
Crown Publishers, Inc.
New York

A Prince Paperback Book
Published by Crown Publishers, Inc., 225 Park Ave-
nue South, New York, New York 10003 and repre-
sented in Canada by the Canadian MANDA Group
CROWN, PRINCE PAPERBACKS, and colophon
are trademarks of Crown Publishers, Inc.
Manufactured in the United States of America
Library of Congress Cataloging in Publication Data

Nash, Bruce M.
  Freebies for cat lovers.

  1. Cats—Equipment and supplies—Catalogs.   2. Free
material—Catalogs.   I. Zullo, Allan.   II. Dieckmann,
Maria E. Grau.   III. Kuh, Ginger.   IV. Title.
SF447.3.N37   1987   636.8   87-8842
ISBN 0-517-56626-5
10 9 8 7 6 5   4   3   2   1
First Edition

Pledge

The companies, organizations, institutions, and associations listed in this book have promised in writing that the items described in *Freebies for Cat Lovers* will be available to readers at a cost to them of no more than $1 (plus any handling and postage costs) through 1988. This guarantee applies to single requests by mail from readers.

Dedication

This book is dedicated to cat lovers everywhere.

Contents

All cats are created equal, but in writing about them in *Freebies for Cat Lovers*, we use "he" and "his" in reference to all cats, regardless of their sex. We have done this for consistency and simplicity.

Introduction

People are discovering what cat lovers have known for a long time: Cats are among the most intelligent, beautiful, playful, and affectionate animal companions ever to win our hearts.

No wonder one out of every four American families shares its home with at least one cat. Each year, cat owners spend about $1.4 billion just on food for their feline friends. Add to that the cost of cat toys, litter box fillers, countless accessories, and veterinary care, and you can better understand why we spend so much on our cats.

Of course, it's worth every penny. But it's also nice to find inexpensive ways to make life with your cat more enjoyable and rewarding.

That's why we've compiled *Freebies for Cat Lovers*. It's a marvelous collection of over two hundred free and up-to-a-dollar items available through the mail for cats and their owners. In this book, you will find descriptions of informative booklets, pamphlets, and guides on such subjects as health, safety, nutrition, and general cat care; toys, accessories, treats, and food samples for your cat; copies of newsletters and magazines from cat organizations; cat-theme novelties to show off your love for felines; product samples and mail-order catalogs—all of which you can obtain for the cost of a postage stamp or a little more. Leafing through these pages will give you access to information, services, and products—everything you need to help you become a better cat owner.

To put this book together, we solicited items from hundreds of organizations, institutions, companies, and associations. Then we evaluated every item that we received and selected those we considered to be the best offers.

The suppliers listed in this book are eager to spread good will about their products, services, or causes by disseminating information at little or no cost or by offering free samples. We want to thank them for their cooperation in making this book possible.

1

How to Send for Your Freebie

- Follow the directions given in the listing and type or legibly print your request.
- Ask for only one copy of each item unless the listing allows for multiple orders.
- Make each request as brief as possible.
- Send a postcard whenever possible unless directions say otherwise. Postcards will save you money on postage.
- When directions call for an envelope, state in your request letter exactly what you are enclosing, such as the amount of money or a self-addressed, stamped envelope. Better yet, photocopy and use the sample request form found on the next page.
- Write your name and address both on the envelope and on the request letter.
- When sending money, use the fewest number of coins possible and tape them to your request letter so they are less likely to fall out if the envelope is accidently ripped.
- If a self-addressed, stamped envelope is required, fold and enclose a standard business envelope (usually 9 or 10 inches long).
- Be prepared to wait four to six weeks for your items to arrive. Your request may be answered sooner, but you may also have to wait a little longer if a particular supplier receives many requests.

Sample Order Form

Use the handy request form below to send away for freebies in this
book. Make photocopies of the form, and then print or type the date,
the item you are requesting, your name, and your address. Also check
the appropriate box and, if necessary, fill in the amount of money you
are enclosing.

. . . .

Date————————————————

Hello!

Please send me the following item(s) listed in *Freebies for Cat Lovers*
(Crown Publishers, Inc., New York):

———————————————————————————

———————————————————————————

I have enclosed:

   □ a self-addressed, stamped business envelope
   □————— to cover the cost of the item and/or postage and
handling

Name————————————————————————
Address—————————————————————————
City————————————— State————— Zip—————

PLAYTHINGS

Sid the Squid

This toy consists of a bright colored ball made of furry material and six leather "tentacles." Sid the Squid has black eyes. Your cat will enjoy making the toy roll and wiggle on the floor.

Send: $1.00 plus 25¢ postage and handling
Ask for: Sid the Squid
Write to: Wendon Corporation 6515 South McKinley Avenue Los Angeles, CA 90001

Cat Fish Toy

Yes, this is truly a "cat fish"—a felt fish that is sure to give your pet a swimmingly good time. The toy is made to withstand hard playing without falling apart. Best of all, your cat will love this fish because it is stuffed with catnip.

Send: $1.00 plus 50¢ postage and handling
Ask for: Cat Fish Toy
Write to: Cats, Cats & More Cats
P.O. Box 270-FF
Monroe, NY 10950

Jungle Fur Paw

The Jungle Fur Paw is a cute 3-by-2-inch oval pillow with fur on one side and beige felt on the other. A bell is attached to the pillow with a small golden chain. This toy's texture and sound will keep your cat entertained for hours.

Send: $1.00
Ask for: Jungle Fur Paw
Write to: Satra's Purr Palace
Route 1, Box 21
Whitewater, WI 53190

Catnip Critter

This adorable cat toy is handmade with fabric that has been prewashed to remove all chemicals. The 4-by-3½-inch oval pillow is stuffed with organically grown catnip. The Catnip Critter is completely safe—it has no parts that can be pulled off and swallowed. It is easily held in a cat's paws, and the material will not tear when your feline chews on it.

    Send: $1.00
  Ask for: Catnip Critter
 Write to: The Catnip Corner
          P.O. Box 2481
          Youngstown, OH 44509

Gooney Bird

Not only sounds and smells but also colors can entice and hold a cat's interest. The Gooney Bird is a multicolored toy made of durable nylon, with special holes to allow the scent of catnip inside to escape. The Gooney Bird can be hung from a cord so it can be swatted by your pet.

    Send: $1.00 plus 25¢ postage and handling
  Ask for: Gooney Bird
 Write to: Wendon Corporation
          6515 South McKinley Avenue
          Los Angeles, CA 90001

Raz-berry Carpet Tumbler

If you are looking for a funny toy companion for your cat, get the Raz-berry Carpet Tumbler for him to bat around. It's a small ball of nylon carpeting with big black plastic google eyes and a leather tongue that hangs out of its tiny mouth. The carpet tumbler comes in a variety of colors.

Send: $1.00 plus 25¢ postage and handling
Ask for: Raz-berry Carpet Tumbler
Write to: Wendon Corporation
6515 South McKinley Avenue
Los Angeles, CA 90001

Crocheted Catnip Mouse

Why not crochet a catnip mouse for your favorite feline? Pennywise Patterns offers a cute pattern with easy-to-follow directions that even include a photo of the finished item. You can make the crocheted mouse from scraps of gray and black yarn and fill it with catnip. The mouse takes only a few minutes to complete and will provide hours of enjoyment for your pet.

Send: 50¢
Ask for: Catnip Mouse Crochet Pattern
Write to: Pennywise Patterns
P.O. Box 119—Department C
Bemus Point, NY 14712

Willie Worm

This toy is made of bright colored balls of a tear-resistant fake-fur material. Sporting a cute face with big black eyes, Willie Worm coils up like a giant worm. Its lively color scheme will have even the laziest of felines up and playing.

Send: $1.00 plus 25¢ postage and handling
Ask for: Willie Worm
Write to: Wendon Corporation
6515 South McKinley Avenue
Los Angeles, CA 90001

Calico Catnip Pouch

Looking for a cute little gift for your cat or cat-lover friend? A calico catnip pouch could be just the thing. This little calico bag is tied with colorful yarn and a bell. It's filled with Super Sausalito catnip—all blossoms and leaves, no twigs or fillers—that was grown in California.

Send: $1.00
Ask for: Calico Catnip Pouch
Write to: Cats, Cats & More Cats
P.O. Box 270-FF
Monroe, NY 10950
Catnip Bag Toy

Catnip Bag Toy

Cheer up your finicky pussy and keep him entertained with this burlap bag filled with catnip. It's a fun toy to kick around, and it's guaranteed to hold your kitty's attention.

Send: $1.00
Ask for: Catnip Bag Toy
Write to: Wendon Corporation
6515 South McKinley Avenue
Los Angeles, CA 90001

FOOD
AND TREATS

Freeze-Dried Tidbits

These bite-sized, freeze-dried tidbits come in liver, fish, or fish and chicken flavor, are 100 percent natural and contain no additives or preservatives. They have the same color, aroma, flavor, and nutritional value as the fresh, raw, natural product. Packaged in handy bags, they are easy to carry in a pocket or purse since they require no refrigeration. The purr-fect treat to keep your cat content at home, while you are waiting at the vet's office, or traveling.

Send: $1.00
Ask for: freeze-dried liver treats, fish treats, or fish and chicken treats for cats
Write to: Redi Industries Corp.
301 Peninsula Boulevard
Hempstead, NY 11550

Natural Cat Food

Every loving cat owner worries about the minimal nutritional value and harmful chemicals present in some pet foods on the market. Cornucopia Super Stars Natural Cat Foods offers a balanced diet for both kittens and cats. The product comes canned or dried and is loaded with nutrients and proteins to help improve your feline's overall health through a proper diet. Preserved naturally with vitamin C and vitamin E, this natural food is chemical free, with no added sugar, artificial preservatives, additives, or colorings.

Send: $1.00
Ask for: sampler of both canned and dry Cornucopia Super Stars Natural Cat Foods
Write to: Cornucopia Veterinary Nutritional Associates, Ltd.
229 Wall Street
Huntington, NY 11743

Protein Supplement

Protein is important for your cat's coat and general health. You can get a one-ounce sample of a protein supplement called Pro-Magic. It's an all-natural protein powder that's easy to digest and can be added wet or dry to your kitty's regular food.

Send: $1.00
Ask for: sample of Pro-Magic
Write to: American Nutritional Laboratories
109 Elbow Lane
Burlington, NJ 08016

Cat Snap Treats

Spoil your kitty with a treat that is filled with natural vitamins and minerals not always available in his daily food. Cat Snap Treats are tasty morsels that he can't resist. Giving these treats, which promote a healthy and glossy coat, is a wonderful way to reward your pet for being good.

Send: $1.00
Ask for: sample of Cat Snap Treats
Write to: Losvet
P.O. Box 2473
Beverly Hills, CA 90213

Liver-Flavored Treats

Let your cat indulge to his heart's content in a free sample of liver-flavored Pet Treats, the healthy snack especially designed to increase an animal's utilization of protein as much as 50 percent by establishing the amino acid balance needed for maximum protein assimilation. It also provides vitamins A, B complex, C, D, E, and K, and minerals such as calcium, iron, manganese, and zinc. It is rich in carotene, a substance that helps strengthen cell membranes against invasive cancer cells. This completely natural food is fortified with brewer's yeast and garlic to keep your pet's skin and tissues healthy.

Send: a postcard
Ask for: free sample of liver-flavored Pet Treats
Write to: EcoSafe Laboratories
Herbal Animal Division
P.O. Box 8702
Oakland, CA 94662

Edible Greens

Cats need greens in their diet. Deprived of this vital part of their nutritional intake, they will sometimes chew on house plants—often with uncomfortable or fatal results. Now, with these seeds, you can grow edible, sweet-tasting grass that is healthy for your cat. Both indoor and outdoor kitties will nibble with delight on the tender green spears. The seeds come in bags, each containing enough for two crops.

Send: $1.00 plus a 22¢ stamp
Ask for: edible greens seeds
Write to: Exotic Seed & Nursery
Route 2, Box 1690
Norridgewock, ME 04957

Dry Cat Food

Dry cat food is more convenient and tidier than canned food. It leaves no messy bowls and does not spoil as fast. This food for the domestic feline is formulated with a high nutritional density, so that the average eight-pound cat need consume only about two ounces per day to receive an adequate nutritional intake.

Send: a postcard
Ask for: sample of Science Diet Domestic Feline Maintenance Food
Write to: Hill's Pet Products, Inc.
P.O. Box 148
Topeka, KS 66601

Wild Oats

If your pussy has digestive problems it may be because he's not getting enough tender greens in his system. Greens are nature's way of providing chlorophyll, vitamins, and minerals for your cat. Now you can get a 2½-ounce bag of wild oat seeds that you can easily grow at home in seven days. Each bag contains twelve plantings.

Send: $1.00
Ask for: wild oats
Write to: Wendon Corporation
6515 South McKinley Avenue
Los Angeles, CA 90001

Catnip Cookies

Famous Fonzworth, a division of the well-known Famous Fido's Doggie Deli, presents the ultimate catnip cookie: a "Feline Fritter." This morsel of fish and catnip herbs is freshly baked with all-natural ingredients. Send now for your sample of three heart-shaped cookies, which come in a designer paper bag.

Send: $1.00
Ask for: catnip cookies sample
Write to: Famous Fido's, Inc.
1527 West Devon
Chicago, IL 60660

Catnip Seeds

You don't have to buy catnip—you can grow it. Exotic Seed & Nursery Co. offers a kit that includes instructions and enough catnip seeds for many years of growing. You can let your cat nibble on the leaves of a live plant or feed him crumbled-up pieces of dried catnip. Either way, your feline will be in seventh heaven.

Send: $1.00 plus a 22¢ stamp
Ask for: catnip seeds
Write to: Exotic Seed & Nursery
Route 2, Box 1690
Norridgewock, ME 04957

Cosmic Catnip Garden

Now you can have a catnip garden right in your own home. United Pharmacal Company offers a colorful polybag containing two pre-planted starters of a special strain of catnip, Cosmic Catnip.

Send: $1.00
Ask for: Cosmic Catnip
Write to: United Pharmacal Company, Inc.
3705 Pear Street
P.O. Box 969
St. Joseph, MO 64502

Catnip Packet

Have you ever considered treating your kitty to home-grown catnip rather than the store-bought variety? From Taylor's Herb Garden you can obtain a packet of seeds, including instructions on how to plant and care for this tasty plant that cats crave.

Send: $1.00
Ask for: packet of catnip seeds
Write to: Taylor's Herb Garden, Inc.
1535 Lone Oak Road
Vista, CA 92083

NUTRITION AND HEALTH

First Aid

If you were faced with the problem of an injured or seriously ill cat, would you know what to do for your pet? Angell Memorial—one of the country's leading animal hospitals—has produced a thorough guide to animal first aid. It tells you how to recognize symptoms of injury or illness; how to restrain a sick cat; how to transport it; how to recognize the symptoms of snake bite, electrical shock, and poisoning; how to administer liquids; how to apply a pressure bandage and a tourniquet; and how to give artificial respiration. This twenty-page booklet will help you to be prepared.

Send: $1.00
Ask for: *Angell Memorial Guide to Animal First Aid*
Write to: Massachusetts Society for the
          Prevention of Cruelty to Animals
          Publication Department
          350 South Huntington Avenue
          Boston, MA 02130
          Attention: Elizabeth Stevens

Nutritional Supplement

K-zyme supplement is based on an enzyme-producing culture blended with amino acids, multivitamins, minerals, two live yeast cultures, and brewer's yeast. It provides more than twenty different types of enzymes that work with the cat's digestive system to increase the utilization and absorption of nutrients and to improve the skin and hair. This product contains no drugs, chemicals, or synthetic compounds.

Send: a postcard
Ask for: free sample of K-zyme for cats
Write to: Bio-zyme Enterprises, Inc.
1231 Alabama, P.O. Box 428
St. Joseph, MO 64504

Feline Nutrition Pamphlet

Nutrition is a key factor in promoting the good health, performance, and longevity of your cat. Your feline will be what you feed it. This pamphlet provides answers to the most common questions cat owners are faced with when considering their kitties' dietary needs: Is a low-ash diet healthy? Are dry foods better for a cat's teeth? Are additives and preservatives dangerous?

Send: a postcard
Ask for: *Feline Nutrition*
Write to: Hill's Pet Products, Inc.
P.O. Box 148
Topeka, KS 66601

Ash-Free Cat Food

An excess of minerals, particularly magnesium, in your cat's diet can cause a disease called Feline Urological Syndrome (F.U.S.). F.U.S. is nothing to sniff at—it accounts for 10 percent of all feline veterinary hospital admissions. The total mineral content of a food as determined by laboratory analysis is called ash. This bulletin tells you about ash and the role it plays in promoting or damaging the health of your feline.

Send: a postcard
Ask for: *There Are No Ashes in Cat Food*
Write to: Hill's Pet Products, Inc.
P.O. Box 148
Topeka, KS 66601

Nutrition and Nurture

This sixty-eight-page booklet, written by veterinarians Mark L. Morris, Jr., and Lon D. Lewis, discusses the care and feeding of cats and dogs. Subjects include the optimal amounts of nutrients needed in a diet, types and forms of pet foods and how to determine their quality, feeding methods, the amount to feed, care and feeding during stress and exertion, and diets for each stage of your pet's life.

Send: $1.00
Ask for: *Feeding Dogs and Cats*
Write to: Mark Morris Associates
5500 S.W. 7th Street
Topeka, KS 66606

Facts about Disease

This useful brochure helps the cat owner understand his cat's illness. It points out the importance of paying attention to symptoms like sneezing and fever as a means of diagnosing feline disorders, describes rhinotracheitis, calicivirus, chlamydia psittaci, panleukopenia, and rabies in detail, and explains about the vaccines that can prevent some of these diseases entirely.

Send: a self-addressed, stamped business envelope
Ask for: *Disease Facts Every Cat Owner Should Know*
Write to: Coopers Animal Health, Inc.
P.O. Box 419167
Kansas City, MO 64141

Respiratory Infection

Since respiratory infections prevent your cat from smelling food, he often does not eat until his sense of smell is restored. This may cause stress, malnutrition, and dehydration. This flyer will give you helpful information about respiratory infections and how they can be treated.

Send: a self-addressed, stamped business envelope
Ask for: *Solution to Respiratory Problems for Cats*
Write to: Professional Pet Products, Inc.
1873 N.W. 97th Avenue
Miami, FL 33172

Assessing Animal Hospitals

This circular put out by the American Animal Hospital Association lists the qualities you should look for in an animal hospital: accurate record keeping, complete diagnostic capabilities, proper anesthetic procedures, and modern surgical facilities. It also discusses the importance of dental services, nursing care, emergency care, and complete pharmaceutical facilities.

Send: a self-addressed, stamped business envelope
Ask for: *We Know How Much You Care . . .*
Write to: American Animal Hospital Association
Department PRNZ
P.O. Box 15899
Denver, CO 80215–0899

Facts about Worms

"Worms" is a generalized term for internal parasites. These nasty little creatures can damage body tissue and produce toxic substances that can harm your cat. They can also suck blood and cause anemia. You can learn more about worms and how to combat them by reading this pamphlet offered by the Oregon Veterinary Medical Association.

Send: a postcard
Ask for: *Facts about Worms*
Write to: Oregon Veterinary Medical Association
1880 Lancaster Drive N.E.
Suite 118
Salem, OR 97305

External Parasites

If you find your cat scratching frequently, discover bald spots, or notice that his skin is inflamed, chances are he is playing host to some external parasites, such as fleas or mites. This brochure discusses different types of external parasites and what to do to rid your cat of these pesky guests. There are sections devoted to fleas, lice, mites, earmites, mange, and ticks.

Send: a self-addressed, stamped business envelope
Ask for: *What You Should Know about External Parasites*
Write to: American Veterinary Medical Association
930 North Meacham Road
Schaumburg, IL 60196

Internal Parasites

This folded circular discusses the principal types of worms and protozoa that can affect your pet's health. It lists the symptoms caused by internal parasites—change in appetite, coughing, diarrhea, and bloody stools—and points out the benefits of fast action and periodic examinations to determine whether parasites have been eliminated.

Send: a self-addressed, stamped business envelope
Ask for: *Internal Parasites*
Write to: American Animal Hospital Association
Department PRNZ
P.O. Box 15899
Denver, CO 80215–0899

Health Record

It's annoying and embarrassing when you take your kitty to the vet only to discover that you are unable to answer pertinent questions about his health history. This useful health record will help you keep all this information properly organized. There is a chart with room for you to jot down your cat's medical history, vaccination records, and details about accidents or illnesses. There is even a space in which to paste a picture of your kitty to assist in identification in case he ever gets lost.

Send: a self-addressed, stamped business envelope
Ask for: *My Cat's Health Record*
Write to: Carnation Company
Pet Care Center
P.O. Box 220, Department F
Pico Rivera, CA 90665

Health Exams

An ounce of prevention is worth a pound of cure. This is as true for the health of your pet as it is for any member of your family. This folded circular contains information about what to expect when you visit the veterinarian with your cat. It also points out some of the most common symptoms of disease. A wet nose, scratching the ears, or changes in the retina may indicate health problems. An examination of the gums and teeth could reveal anemia, and the condition of the skin —for example, if it's tight and dry—could also indicate the onset of illness. The brochure also points out the benefits of immunization.

Send: a self-addressed, stamped business envelope
Ask for: *Health Exams*
Write to: American Animal Hospital Association
Department PRNZ
P.O. Box 15899
Denver, CO 80215–0899

Medical History

Your cat deserves the best health care possible. This informative cat-care booklet helps you keep track of your pet's medical history. It includes a handy form where you can list your cat's vaccinations and immunizations, worming, illnesses, visits to the veterinarian, and other records. The booklet also contains sections on fleas, overweight cats, introducing a second cat into the house, and training and exercising your cat.

Send: $1.00
Ask for: *Cat Care*
Write to: Massachusetts Society for the
      Prevention of Cruelty to Animals
      Publication Department
      350 South Huntington Avenue
      Boston, MA 02130
      Attention: Elizabeth Stevens

Health Program

A basic health program for cats is relatively simple and inexpensive. It involves three to four visits to the veterinarian in your kitten's first year, then a yearly visit during the cat's adult life. But don't leave all the work in the hands of the veterinarian. You can learn to recognize the symptoms of feline diseases with the help of this booklet. It also contains information about spaying, neutering, and vaccinations.

Send: 25¢
Ask for: *A Basic Health Program for Your Cat*
Write to: The American Society for the
      Prevention of Cruelty to Animals
      441 East 92nd Street
      New York, NY 10128

Preventing Contagious Diseases

Your cat is susceptible to a wide range of diseases, but proper vaccination can protect him from many of the most serious. This free pamphlet explains the common contagious diseases and how they can be prevented. It also has a handy immunization form to help you keep track of your cat's vaccinations.

Send: a postcard
Ask for: *Contagious Diseases*
Write to: Oregon Veterinary Medical Association
1880 Lancaster Drive N.E.
Suite 118
Salem, OR 97305

Feline Disease

Your greatest wish as a cat owner is a long, healthy life for your animal companion. Yet a great many cats become victims of the many viruses and health problems, such as feline leukemia, that affect the species. This pamphlet will inform you about the latest research advances in the field of feline disease, from the discovery of new viruses to the development of new treatments and vaccines.

Send: a postcard
Ask for: *Feline Health*
Write to: Morris Animal Foundation
45 Inverness Drive East
Englewood, CO 80112

Symptoms of Disease

Veterinarian Jay Kuhlman has put together a list of the symptoms that may indicate your cat has a serious health problem. These include appetite loss, cloudy eyes, constant thirst, drooling, straining to defecate, and any new or growing lumps anywhere on the body. This fact sheet also offers helpful suggestions about ways to keep your cat healthy.

Send: a self-addressed, stamped business envelope
Ask for: *Signs of Serious Problems and Helpful Hints for Healthy Cats*
Write to: Feline and Canine Friends, Inc.
505 North Bush Street
Anaheim, CA 92805

Feline Panleukopenia

If your kitty is showing signs of general depression, loss of appetite, high fever, vomiting, or dehydration, he could be suffering from feline panleukopenia, a highly contagious disease also known as feline distemper. It can strike cats at any age, but it often attacks kittens less than sixteen weeks old, usually with fatal results. Be prepared to recognize the symptoms of this deadly disease with this pamphlet put out by the American Veterinary Medical Association. Your awareness may save your kitty's life.

Send: a self-addressed, stamped business envelope
Ask for: *What You Should Know about Feline Panleukopenia*
Write to: American Veterinary Medical Association
930 North Meacham Road
Schaumburg, IL 60196

Learning about Feline Leukemia

Should you be concerned about feline leukemia virus? The answer is yes, particularly if you have more than one cat or kitten, or if your pet has frequent contact with other cats or kittens. This disease is highly contagious and affects cats of all ages, although it does not affect humans or other species. Learn more about this serious virus from this pamphlet, which answers some of the most common questions cat owners ask.

    Send: a self-addressed, stamped business envelope
  Ask for: *Feline Leukemia Virus*
Write to: American Animal Hospital Association
           Department PRNZ
           P.O. Box 15899
           Denver, CO 80215–0899

Feline Urological Syndrome

Feline Urological Syndrome (F.U.S.) is a typical problem in cats. Its exact cause is still unknown; however, this pamphlet provides you with details about the most common types of F.U.S.—cystitis, urolithiasis, urethral blockage, and uremia. It also provides information about treatment and gives tips on how to avoid the syndrome.

    Send: a self-addressed, stamped business envelope
  Ask for: *Feline Urological Syndrome*
Write to: American Animal Hospital Association
           Department PRNZ
           P.O. Box 15899
           Denver, CO 80215–0899

Learning More about F.U.S.

If you want to know all the clinical aspects of Feline Urological Syndrome, then send for this detailed thirty-nine-page booklet written by two specialists in the field. The booklet, complete with charts and tables, discusses clinical signs, diagnoses, causes, treatments, and preventive measures related to this disease, common among cats.

Send: $1.00
Ask for: *Feline Urological Syndrome*
Write to: Mark Morris Associates
5500 S.W. 7th Street
Topeka, KS 66606

Rabies Poster

This full-color 24-by-18-inch poster clearly explains, with text and illustrations, important information about rabies. It answers the most common questions about this disorder: What is rabies? How does the disease spread? How do you know if an animal has rabies? What can be done if your pet has rabies? How can rabies be prevented?

Send: a postcard
Ask for: "What You Should Know About Rabies" poster
Write to: Barbara Johnson
Shering Animal Health
1011 Morris Avenue
Union, NJ 07083

A Clean Mouth

Does your cat have bad breath? If so, it could be caused by a poor diet or be a sign of disease. According to this bulletin, you should make sure that your cat is eating a high-protein diet and has plenty of fresh water to drink. The bulletin also offers tips on proper dental hygiene for your cat.

Send: a postcard
Ask for: *On a Clean Mouth*
Write to: Oregon Veterinary Medical Association
1880 Lancaster Drive N.E.
Suite 118
Salem, OR 97305

Dental Care

Oral hygiene is just as important for your pet as it is for members of the family. Bad teeth and periodontal and gum diseases plague pets, too. This brochure provides information on how to brush your pet's teeth and discusses other tooth-related diseases that may affect your pet.

Send: a self-addressed, stamped business envelope
Ask for: *Dental Care*
Write to: American Animal Hospital Association
Department PRNZ
P.O. Box 15899
Denver, CO 80215–0899

SAFETY

Cold Weather Tips

Winter is tough for both you and your feline. Cats who are lost or stolen when it's cold out can easily freeze to death, and even indoors, cold is a hazard. This bulletin offers twelve easy ways to protect your cat from low temperatures, among them keeping him inside and increasing his supply of food, especially protein, to keep his fur thick and healthy.

Send: a postcard
Ask for: *Cold Weather Tips* bulletin
Write to: American Society for the
Prevention of Cruelty to Animals
441 East 92nd Street
New York, NY 10128

Poison Prevention

Cat owners should be aware of the variety of poisons that are potentially dangerous to their pets and the ways in which cats can come in contact with them. This useful brochure lists some of the more common poisons—such as arsenic and cyanide—and how they will affect the animal who ingests them. There is also a section devoted to indirect chemical poisoning, which may occur when your cat eats the remains of a poisoned rodent or bird, or when a playful kitty nibbles on a poisonous plant. The brochure offers rules to follow in order to prevent your animal from being poisoned, such as knowing where he is at all times, and advises on what to do in case of poisoning.

Send: 50¢ plus a self-addressed, stamped envelope
Ask for: *Protecting Pets from Household Poisons*
Write to: The American Humane Association
P.O. Box 1266
Denver, CO 80201

Lost Pet Poster

Losing a pet is a frightening experience. The key to finding your cat is quick and effective action, so be prepared with this lost pet poster. This 8½-by-11-inch poster has sections for all pertinent information and even has a place to display a photo of your cat. Once it's filled out, you can make photocopies and pass them out around your neighborhood.

Send: 50¢ postage and handling
Ask for: lost pet poster for cats
Write to: Tatoo-A-Pet
1625 Emmons Avenue
Brooklyn, NY 11235

Water for Your Pet

It is a common misconception that felines love milk and will never go near water. Nothing could be further from the truth. In fact, one key to good health for your pet is a constant supply of fresh water. This bulletin teaches you how to keep your pet safely supplied with fresh water and shows the dangers of drinking dirty water, which attracts flies and mosquitoes and fosters bacterial disease. Among other things, it reminds you to wash your pet's dish daily and to take along a thermos of cool water when traveling with him.

Send: a postcard
Ask for: *Fresh Water* bulletin
Write to: American Society for the
Prevention of Cruelty to Animals
441 East 92nd Street
New York, NY 10128

Hot Weather Tips

Those sunny summer days are glorious, but according to this bulletin, they could also represent a hazard to your pet. For example, did you ever stop to think that the garden you just sprayed with insecticide could poison a cat romping on the grass? Other things to remember: never leave your pet in a car; always provide plenty of cool, clean water; never let your cat out to run loose; always keep a current license and identification tag on your pet; never take your pet to the beach; and watch out for fleas and ticks.

Send: a postcard
Ask for: *Hot Weather Tips* bulletin
Write to: American Society for the
Prevention of Cruelty to Animals
441 East 92nd Street
New York, NY 10128

Keep Your Cat Indoors

The dangers that lurk outside the house, from careless drivers to para-sites, worms, rabies, and infestations, make it impractical and sense-less for your feline companion to roam freely. This magazine article reprint outlines these potential hazards and offers tips on how to pre-serve your kitty's health by keeping him indoors. It demonstrates con-vincingly that cats kept indoors live longer and happier lives.

Send: 25¢
Ask for: *Keep Your Cat Indoors*
Write to: The Humane Society of the United States
2100 L Street, N.W.
Washington, DC 20037

Fire Rescue Decal

Thousands of pets die annually as a result of fire and other domestic disasters. Fire departments and emergency personnel have indicated a willingness to rescue pets when made aware of their existence. This bright label can be permanently affixed to doors or windows and shows the number and type of pets that are on the premises. It measures 3 by 3 inches, is self-adhesive, and has white letters on a red background.

Send: $1.00
Ask for: two pet fire rescue decals
Write to: Friends of Animals
1 Pine Street
Neptune, NJ 07753

34

Make Me-Ow Safe

You can use the Poly Tie-Out rope to keep your kitty near the house and safe from careless drivers when he's playing outside. Each end of the sturdy 10-foot nylon rope contains a bolt snap. Attach one of the bolt snaps to your cat's collar and put the other bolt snap on a clothes line. As the bolt snap slides along the clothes line, the rope gives your cat enough room to play—but prevents him from getting into trouble.

Send: $1.00 plus 50¢ postage and handling
Ask for: 10-foot Poly Tie-Out with bolt snaps
Write to: Vest Products
5970 Jaycox Road
North Ridgeville, OH 44039

Nylon Collar

If you are a responsible pet owner, you do not want your cat to roam about without proper identification. This handy ⅜-inch collar will ensure that identification tags are securely attached to your feline. The collar is 100-percent nylon and comes in several lengths—8, 10, 12, and 14 inches. There are nine colors to choose from: red, blue, brown, black, green, tan, orange, orchard, and light blue.

Send: $1.00 plus 25¢ postage and handling
Ask for: nylon collar (state size and color)
Write to: Vest Products
5970 Jaycox Road
North Ridgeville, OH 44039

Finding Your Lost Cat

Thousands of cats disappear every year. Whether lost, strayed, or stolen, the result is the same—your kitty is without you and you are heartbroken. Do not panic. Be prepared with this handy booklet. Learn what to do if your cat is lost: who to contact and what steps to take to recover your pet.

Send: a postcard
Ask for: *What to Do if Your Pet Is Lost*
Write to: Tatoo-A-Pet
       1625 Emmons Avenue
       Brooklyn, NY 11235

Tattoo ID

Thousands of pet owners have already discovered a new and effective way to protect their pets in case they get lost or stolen—by tattooing an individual number on the animal. The procedure is quick and painless and provides a permanent method of identification. The number is fed into a computer with your name, address, and telephone number, and anyone who finds your lost or stolen kitty can call a toll-free telephone number so you can be notified immediately. A brochure and cassette describe the service in detail and outline the advantages of protecting your cat through tattooing.

Send: 50¢ postage and handling
Ask for: free brochure and audiocassette on tattooing to protect your cat
Write to: Tatoo-A-Pet
       1625 Emmons Avenue
       Brooklyn, NY 11235

I Brake for Animals

Remind the driver behind you to watch out for our feline friends on the streets of your neighborhood. You can call attention to cat safety with this cute bumper sticker, which reads: "I Brake for Animals."

Send: $1.00 plus 65¢ postage and handling
Ask for: "I Brake for Animals" bumper sticker
Write to: Tru-Beauty Distributors
760 East Park Lane
Columbia, MO 65201

Death Trap

Cat lovers really get their dander up when they spot a pet locked inside an unattended car parked in the sun with the windows rolled up. It takes only a few minutes for the temperature inside to soar up to as high as 130 degrees—enough to kill a healthy cat, or at the very least cause heat prostration.
If you see this sickening sight, call the local animal rescue league—and then place under the windshield wiper this notice, which tells the miscreant owner about the dangers of leaving an animal in a car in hot weather.

Send: 50¢ plus a self-addressed, stamped business envelope
Ask for: "Deadly Mistake" notices (ten per order)
Write to: San Diego Humane Society
887 Sherman Street
San Diego, CA 92110

FLEA CONTROL AND GROOMING

Grooming

Cats are naturally tidy and usually keep themselves clean and groomed. However, a little help from you is always appreciated. This pamphlet offers tips on brushing and combing your pet and bathing him on those rare occasions when he's so dirty he can't clean himself, as well as sensible suggestions on cat care. For example, it advises that the best way to clean your cat's ears is with a cotton-tipped applicator moistened with mineral oil.

Send: a postcard
Ask for: *Cat Care*
Write to: The American Feline Society
204 West 20th Street
New York, NY 10011

Fleas

The flea is a hardy adversary with a life span of nine months. During that time, a pair of fleas and a lot of luck could produce an estimated 222 trillion relatives. Fleas are tough! In order to win the battle against them, your cat will need your help. This pamphlet tells you how to conduct a fast and easy test to determine if your cat has fleas and how to "de-flea" him if he has them.

Send: a self-addressed, stamped business envelope
Ask for: *Fleas*
Write to: American Animal Hospital Association
           Department PRNZ
           P.O. Box 15899
           Denver, CO 80215–0899

Flea Control Bulletin

Much more than a nuisance, fleas can cause serious skin diseases, weight loss, and restlessness. And the problem can spread beyond your cat; your house and yard can also become infested. This bulletin gives you some facts about fleas and how they reproduce and describes different methods of fighting these nasty insects.

Send: a self-addressed, stamped business envelope
Ask for: *Flea Problems and How to Control Them*
Write to: Feline and Canine Friends, Inc.
           505 North Bush Street
           Anaheim, CA 92805

Guide to Flea and Tick Control

This illustrated booklet gives pet owners general information about fleas and ticks and what steps to take to make sure household animals are free from this annoyance. It explains how fleas and ticks live and reproduce, what their life cycles are, and where they can be found. A control program is outlined, including tips on how to groom your pet using shampoos, dusting powder, or sprays, how to use foggers in the house, and how to treat pet bedding and yards to eliminate these parasites.

Send: a self-addressed, stamped business envelope
Ask for: *Pet Owners' Guide to Flea and Tick Control*
Write to: Coopers Animal Health, Inc.
P.O. Box 419167
Kansas City, MO 64141

Herbal Flea Collar

Many cats cannot tolerate the harsh chemical flea collars that are currently on the market. Some cats have actually died from the use of these collars. Protect your kitty's health with natural collars. This one is made of cotton cord and treated with essential oils, including pennyroyal, eucalyptus, and cedarwood, that have been used medicinally by herbalists and naturalists for centuries. This collar both reduces the number of fleas on your pet and imparts a pleasant herbal fragrance to his fur.

Send: $1.00
Ask for: herbal flea collar
Write to: Natural Research People, Inc.
South Rte., Box 12
Lavina, MT 59046

Natural Flea and Tick Collar

This 100-percent-natural flea and tick collar is made with an effective, nonirritating blend of flea-control herbs that gives off a delightful scent. It is particularly designed for felines who cannot withstand the harsh chemicals in some commercial flea and tick collars. The collar is made of cotton in a calico print.

Send: $1.00 plus 95¢ postage and handling
Ask for: Color and Herbal Works cat collar (specify small or regular size)
Write to: Color and Herbal Works, Inc.
P.O. Box 1574
Sedona, AZ 86336

Grooming Brush

If you have a long-haired cat, then you know you must brush him often. Not all brushes can get out the tangles without causing your feline friend discomfort. However, brushing can be a joy with this sturdy plastic grooming brush specially designed for long-haired pets.

Send: $1.00
Ask for: grooming brush
Write to: Cat Grooming Brush
Liaho
P.O. Box 176
Peshastin, WA 98847Skin Care

Skin Care

Your cat's skin and coat are often accurate barometers of his general health. Symptoms like scratching, rubbing, or licking may indicate the existence of allergies, bacteria, fungi, parasites, or hormonal problems. This pamphlet gives details about various skin ailments and their treatment.

Send: a self-addressed, stamped business envelope
Ask for: *Skin*
Write to: American Animal Hospital Association
Department PRNZ
P.O. Box 15899
Denver, CO 80215–0899

Secrets of Claw Clipping

A cat's claws grow rapidly, and your cat will scratch the furniture not so much to sharpen his claws as to shorten them. When a cat scratches you in play, it is usually an accident, but you can avoid this by keeping your pet's claws trimmed. This bulletin describes the proper way to trim a cat's claws, and clear illustrations of the structure of a cat's paw and claws make it easy.

Send: a self-addressed, stamped business envelope
Ask for: *Secrets of Claw Clipping*
Write to: Feline and Canine Friends, Inc.
505 North Bush Street
Anaheim, CA 92805

CAT CARE

Why Your Cat Scratches

It's natural for a cat to scratch . . . and it's natural for you to get upset when he does it on your furniture. But before you get too angry, take the time to understand more about scratching. This bulletin explains that cats scratch for several reasons: to stretch their spines and muscles, to shed old claw tissue and sharpen new claws, and to mark their territories.

Send: a self-addressed, stamped business envelope
Ask for: *Why Does Your Cat Scratch?*
Write to: Feline and Canine Friends, Inc.
505 North Bush Street
Anaheim, CA 92805

Don't Declaw Flyer

Home furnishings are expensive, but a cat's well-being is priceless. Your cat should trust you and depend upon you for protection. Don't betray that trust by declawing him. This flyer offers six simple alternatives to declawing, such as using a scratching post, clipping your cat's claws regularly, and punishing your pet with a gentle squirt from a water pistol. These and other inexpensive routines and modifications to your cat's environment can eliminate scratching.

Send: a self-addressed, stamped business envelope
Ask for: *Don't Declaw*
Write to: International Society for Animal Rights, Inc.
421 South State Street
Clarks Summit, PA 18411

Facts about Declawing

In most cases, declawing is a great handicap to a pet cat, and this bulletin explains why. It features a drawing of the ligaments and tendons of a cat's leg and shows the function of the claws, which help cats grasp, hold, establish their footing while walking, and run. The bulletin also discusses the psychological damage and pain cats suffer when declawed.

Send: a self-addressed, stamped business envelope
Ask for: *If You Love Your Cat, Do Not Declaw*
Write to: Feline and Canine Friends, Inc.
505 North Bush Street
Anaheim, CA 92805

Litter Bag

Looking for a clever way to get across an important message and help keep your car clean at the same time? The Associated Humane Societies of New Jersey is offering a plastic litter bag with a drawing of a puppy and a kitty with the words, "Don't litter, spay." With your order you will also receive a free copy of the organization's interesting monthly publication, *Humane News*.

Send: $1.00
Ask for: litter bag
Write to: Associated Humane Societies
124 Evergreen Avenue
Newark, NJ 07114

Cat Care Answers

This booklet answers some of the most common questions asked by cat owners and offers tips on how to care for felines properly. There are sections on feeding, shedding, hairballs, and what to do if a cat becomes lost. Training tips are also featured, and a chapter on health care covers such subjects as feline distemper, fleas, ear mites, and urinary problems.

Send: a self-addressed, stamped business envelope
Ask for: *Cats*
Write to: Pet Care Information
Animal Rescue League of Boston
P.O. Box 265
Boston, MA 02117

A Safe and Happy Home

Cats are naturally inquisitive, and that can sometimes get them into trouble. For this reason, it's important to make your home as safe as possible for your feline friend. In this booklet on general cat care, one section is devoted to precautionary steps you should take to avoid indoor accidents. For example, tuck all dangling cords—whether for lamps, television sets, or telephones—out of your cat's curious reach. He could strangle on a dangling cord or be electrocuted trying to chew through it.

Send: a self-addressed, stamped business envelope
Ask for: *Your Cat's New Home*
Write to: Kal Kan
Dept. C.
P.O. Box 58853
Vernon, CA 90058–0853

Needs and Habits

Cats are easy to care for, but a knowledge of their habits and needs will make the job even easier. This handy brochure discusses subjects such as feeding, health dos and don'ts, housing, common ailments, parasites, and handling and training. There is also a section about simple safety precautions.

Send: 50¢ plus a self-addressed, stamped business envelope
Ask for: *The Care of Cats*
Write to: The American Humane Association
P.O. Box 1266
Denver, CO 80201

Spay Your Pet

Last year the nation's animal shelters had to kill 14 million healthy but unwanted pets. Be kind. Have your cat spayed. This pamphlet will provide you with a list of veterinarians in cities and towns in your state who are participating in the Friends of Animals' Low-cost Spay/Alter Program.

Send: a self-addressed, stamped business envelope
Ask for: "I Want You to Spay Your Pets"
Write to: Friends of Animals, Inc.
1 Pine Street
Neptune, NJ 07753

Housebreaking Your Cat

Housebreaking a cat is seldom a problem, but not all cats are alike. Some may need a little extra patience until they learn the rules of the house. This useful bulletin gives you tips on how to set up a litter box, how to clean it, and how to teach your kitty to use it. It also tells you what to do if your cat continues to make mistakes; for example, you can change the litter more often, try a different kind of litter, or consider the possibility of medical disorders and have your cat examined by a veterinarian.

Send: a postcard
Ask for: *Housebreaking Your Cat*
Write to: American Society for the
Prevention of Cruelty to Animals
441 East 92nd Street
New York, NY 10128

Pethood or Parenthood?

Pets cannot learn to control their mating instincts, and this fact can sometimes interfere with the joy of owning your cat. For example, you may have already endured the nervous pacing and plaintive meowing of a female cat in heat or the angry frustration of your male cat when his mating instincts are blocked. This useful pamphlet details the advantages of surgical neutering and responds to pet owners' most common fears when faced with the decision to neuter—concern about pain, cost, and the quality of life of a neutered cat.

Send: a self-addressed, stamped business envelope
Ask for: *Choose for Your Pet . . . Pethood or Parenthood*
Write to: American Veterinary Medical Association
930 North Meacham Road
Schaumburg, IL 60196

Marmaduke's Story

This bulletin tells the story of a cat named Marmaduke. Marmaduke was destroying himself by trying to win the love of every lady cat. His battles with all the other toms led to savage scratching and some brutal bites. Marmaduke's owner decided to have him neutered, and since then there have been no more problems. Marmaduke's tale is a perfect example of what could happen to your cat if you don't alter him. The bulletin also points out that your cat will be a better companion after being neutered and gives details about the procedure.

Send: a self-addressed, stamped business envelope
Ask for: *Marmaduke*
Write to: Friends of Animals, Inc.
1 Pine Street
Neptune, NJ 07753

A Responsible Choice

As a responsible pet owner you want to ensure your kitty's happiness and good health. One way to do this is to have your cat altered. Remind other motorists and pet owners to keep their animals' well-being in mind with this 11½-by-3-inch bumper sticker which reads, "I ♠ My Pet. Did You?"

Send: 50¢ plus a self-addressed, stamped business envelope
Ask for: "I ♠ My Pet. Did You?" bumper sticker
Write to: Humane Society of Lackawanna County
P.O. Box 229
Clarks Summit, PA 18411

A Plea for Neutering

Animal owners who breed kittens they do not want or do not intend to keep are causing needless feline overpopulation, along with the suffering and death that result from this situation. This flyer gives you facts about abandoned pets and discusses the advantages of neutering your cat, while dispelling myths associated with the procedure, such as the belief that spayed animals develop tumors or become fat and lazy.

Send: a self-addressed, stamped business envelope
Ask for: *A Message to Dog and Cat Owners*
Write to: International Society for Animal Rights, Inc.
421 South State Street
Clarks Summit, PA 18411

SPECIAL SITUATIONS

Traveling Guidelines

Planning and preparation are necessary when traveling with the family cat. This brochure offers suggestions to help minimize the chances of an unpleasant experience if pet owners decide to take their cat with them on a trip. There are sections devoted to travel by air, car, bus, and train. Camping with pets and post-trip examinations are also discussed.

Send: a self-addressed, stamped business envelope
Ask for: *What You Should Know about Traveling with Your Pet*
Write to: American Veterinary Medical Association
930 North Meacham Road
Schaumburg, IL 60196

Raising an Orphan Kitten

This guide describes how to raise an orphan kitten. Its eleven pages cover a wide variety of subjects, including advice on how to provide the right environment for the kitten, the correct temperature for rearing kittens, feeding tips, and information on toilet training. There is also a blank page for notes and a health record in which to note data on illnesses and vaccinations.

Send: a stamped, self-addressed business envelope
Ask for: *The Borden Guide to the Care and Feeding of Orphan Kittens*
Write to: Peg-Ag Inc.
Route 1, Box 127
Elgin, IL 60120

Looking for a Kitten?

Have you been looking for a particular kitten? Maybe you want a special breed or color. Look no more. The Cat Fancier's Data Center provides a free referral service to assist you in locating the nearest breeder member with the breed, sex, and color you are trying to find.

Send: a self-addressed, stamped business envelope
Ask for: cat referral printout (specify the breed you want)
Write to: Cat Fancier's Data Center
77 Essex Avenue
Montclair, NJ 07042

Cat Breed Profile

Learn more about the breed of your cat you are considering getting. The Cat Fancier's Data Center has prepared a brochure on each of thirty different breeds, giving information on their history, physical characteristics, and personality. A free coupon for Step Cat Litter comes with the brochure.

Send: $1.00
Ask for: breed profile (specify breed)
Write to: Cat Fancier's Data Center
77 Essex Avenue
Montclair, NJ 07042

Traveling by Car

Vacation time is here again, and this time you are taking your kitty along. Perhaps you cannot bear to be parted from your pet or you can't afford the expense of boarding him. Whatever the case, this bulletin will give you an idea of what is involved when traveling with your pet by car. It contains ten tips that may help make your auto trip more enjoyable. For example, remember to allow your pet to cater to his needs when you cater to yours; never leave your pet alone in the car; and always carry some packaged moist cat food with you.

Send: a postcard
Ask for: *10 Easy Steps to Remember When Traveling with Your Pet by Car*
Write to: American Society for the
Prevention of Cruelty to Animals
441 East 92nd Street
New York, NY 10128

Allergy-Proofing Your Cat

If you or someone in your family is allergic to your cat, you may not have to give up your pet. There are several easy steps you can take to alleviate the problem and keep pussy around the house. This information booklet explains how to curb your cat's dander—the main cause of humans' allergic reactions to pets—and provides other tips on desensitizing your house.

Send: $1.00
Ask for: *How to Allergy-Proof Your Pet*
Write to: Associated Humane Societies
124 Evergreen Avenue
Newark, NJ 07114

Wills and Bequests

What would happen to your cat if you died or became incapacitated? Give yourself peace of mind by planning ahead. This informative pamphlet explains how to set up your will to arrange for the care of your beloved pet. It also provides guidelines if you wish to make a bequest to an animal shelter.

Send: $1.00
Ask for: Wills and Bequests
Write to: Associated Humane Societies
124 Evergreen Avenue
Newark, NJ 07114

Pleasantly Plump?

Many of America's cats suffer from too much of
the good life. They are fat because they overeat.
Excess fat can lead to heart, liver, and kidney
problems and also put excessive stress on the
joints. Your cat will feel better and happier if you
help him lose weight. This pamphlet offers tips
on creating a weight-loss plan for your cat.

    Send: a postcard
  Ask for: *Pleasantly Plump?*
Write to: Oregon Veterinary Medical Associa-
             tion
             1880 Lancaster Drive N.E.
             Suite 118
             Salem, OR 97305

Your Aging Cat

To their credit, cats age gracefully, complaining only occasionally and
adjusting to their infirmities with a minimum of fuss. However, this is
the time when your cat needs you most. This pamphlet provides you
with information on how you can help your feline live comfortably and
happily throughout his autumn years. It covers subjects such as nutrition and feeding, stress, common ailments, and home care for your sick
cat.

    Send: a self-addressed, stamped business envelope
  Ask for: *Care of Your Aging Cat*
Write to: Carnation Company
             Pet Care Center
             P.O. Box 220, Department F
             Pico Rivera, CA 90665

Euthanasia

Perhaps the kindest thing you can do for a cat that is so sick or severely injured that he will never recover normal health is to have your veterinarian induce death quietly and humanely. This brochure offers suggestions on how to cope with this difficult situation, how to tell your family, how to say goodbye to your cat, and how to face the loss.

Send: a self-addressed, stamped business envelope
Ask for: *Pet Loss and Human Emotion*
Write to: American Veterinary Medical Association
930 North Meacham Road
Schaumburg, IL 60196

How to Find Your Pet

If you suspect your pet is lost, don't run around wildly looking for him. This brochure maps out an efficient strategy for recovering your cat—by following up on leads, printing posters, and contacting your local humane society. It also tells you what *not* to do. For example, you should not be alone when meeting a person who answers your ad for a reward, nor should you tell a stranger the value of your pet. There is also a list of steps to follow to prevent your cat from getting lost in the first place.

Send: a postcard
Ask for: *How to Find Your Pet*
Write to: American Society for the
Prevention of Cruelty to Animals
441 East 92nd Street
New York, NY 10128

Cat Trapping Bulletin

If you want to capture a stray cat so he can receive the proper care he deserves, this bulletin has suggestions on how to do so in a humane way. You can borrow automatic traps from humane organizations in your area, or use a laundry hamper, a cardboard box, or even a big sack with holes punctured in it for ventilation.

Send: a self-addressed, stamped business envelope
Ask for: *Cat Trapping—The Humane Way*
Write to: Feline and Canine Friends, Inc.
505 North Bush Street
Anaheim, CA 92805

Rabies and People

Although in the United States today rabies seldom results in human fatalities, it remains a potentially dangerous public health problem. Each year, more than 20,000 Americans have to undergo anti-rabies treatments as a result of exposure to rabid animals. This brochure gives details about this dreaded viral disease, lists the steps to be taken if you are bitten, and points out what can be done to prevent the spread of rabies.

Send: a self-addressed, stamped business envelope
Ask for: *What You Should Know about Rabies*
Write to: American Veterinary Medical Association
930 North Meacham Road
Schaumburg, IL 60196

Cat Photography

Did you ever struggle to capture the real charm and personality of your cat in a photograph? As those who have attempted to shoot feline pictures will attest, photographing cats—especially independent ones—can be an exasperating experience. This pamphlet describes the best techniques for snapping pictures of your furry friend, including information on equipment needed and tips on focusing.

Send: a self-addressed, stamped business envelope
Ask for: *How to Photograph Your Pet*
Write to: Carnation Company
Pet Care Center
P.O. Box 220, Department F
Pico Rivera, CA 90665

Feline Traveler

Going on a plane and want to take kitty with you? Your feline friend can enjoy a happy and safe trip if you simply make the right preparations. This informative booklet describes the risks of taking a cat on the plane, the precautions you should take, and air-travel rules. In addition, there are sections covering other types of travel situations.

Send: a self-addressed, stamped business envelope
Ask for: *The Traveling Cat & Dog*
Write to: Carnation Company
Pet Care Center
P.O. Box 220, Department F
Pico Rivera, CA 90665

Boarding Your Cat

There are times when you simply can't take your feline friend with you on a trip and must board him. Naturally, you want to minimize the stress that the separation may cause him—and you. The American Boarding Kennels Association has prepared this pamphlet to help you ease your mind and find the best kennel for your cat.

Send: 50¢
Ask for: *Let's Talk about Boarding Your Cat*
Write to: American Boarding Kennels Association
4575 Galley Road
Suite 400-A
Colorado Springs, CO 80915

Pet Memorials

What better way to pay tribute to a faithful friend and companion when he passes away than to mark his burial site with a lovely pet memorial? This information packet provides 110 different designs, any of which can be engraved on the granite of your choice.

Send: a self-addressed, stamped business envelope
Ask for: information packet on pet memorials
Write to: Granite Originals
P.O. Box 6001
Elberton, GA 30635

Shipping Your Cat

If you plan to ship your cat anywhere in the United States or abroad, you certainly need to know the shipping requirements mandated by the Animal Welfare Act. This pamphlet, provided by the Animal Air Transportation Association, discusses the minimum standards for size, ventilation, sanitation, and design of pet containers. At your request, the AATA will also furnish you with a list of certified pet forwarders in your area as well as a brief description of the pertinent laws and regulations that exist in the country where you are shipping your pet.

Send: a self-addressed, stamped business envelope and name of travel destination
Ask for: pet-shipping pamphlet
Write to: AATA
P.O. Box 441110
Fort Washington, MD 20744

Discount Coupons

It's always a delight to receive discounts on items that you plan to buy. Cat Fancier's Data Center, a clearinghouse of information for cat lovers, will send you various discount coupons for such things as products for your feline, admission to cat shows, and subscriptions to various publications.

Send: a self-addressed, stamped business envelope
Ask for: discount coupons
Write to: Cat Fancier's Data Center
77 Essex Avenue
Montclair, NJ 07042

Cat Registration

If you plan to raise kittens for sale, then it is important to register your cats and litter. At your request, The International Cat Association will send you information that explains how to register your cat and/or litter. The association will also provide you with all the proper forms, including one to register your household feline.

Send: a self-addressed, stamped business envelope
Ask for: registration information
Write to: TICA
            P.O. Box 2988
            Harlingen, TX 78551

AROUND THE HOUSE

Rug and Room Deodorizer

Even though you know your kitty's habits are above reproach, sometimes you may need something extra to cover up that faint odor that reveals the presence of a pet in the house. This rug and room deodorizer is a nontoxic, commercial-strength, sprinkle-on, vacuum-up freshener. It can be used on rugs as well as on hard surfaces, furniture, and pet beds.

Send: $1.00
Ask for: Outright Rug and Room Deodorizer sample
Write to: The Bramton Company
P.O. Box 655450
Dallas, TX 75265

Cat Litter Deodorizer

This odor eliminator for the litter box contains two nontoxic active ingredients—an enzyme and a deodorizer. The enzyme acts on the urine, breaking it down into a less noxious form, while the deodorizer instantly produces a pleasant fragrance. To use, simply sprinkle over fresh litter in the box, using two tablespoons for every pound of cat litter. Your cat's natural digging action will help spread the powder through the litter box.

Send: $1.00
Ask for: Outright Odor Eliminator Additive for Cat Litter sample
Write to: The Bramton Company
P.O. Box 655450
Dallas, TX 75265

Detergent-Deodorizer

Nilosol is specially designed for pet owners who want to keep their pet areas and cages looking and smelling clean. This product performs double duty by cleaning and deodorizing all washable surfaces. Because it contains no harsh alkalis, acids, or toxic disinfectants, it can be used safely around your cat.

Send: $1.00
Ask for: two-ounce Nilosol sample
Write to: Nilodor, Inc.
7740 Freedom Avenue, N.W.
North Canton, OH 44720

Odor Neutralizer

This odor neutralizer, in pipette form, is a superconcentrated and non-toxic aid for cat lovers who want to enjoy their pets without having to put up with feline odors. One drop of fluid daily will deodorize a 10-by-10-foot room and exude a minty-pine scent.

Send: $1.00
Ask for: 25-S Nilodor pipette
Write to: Nilodor, Inc.
7740 Freedom Avenue, N.W.
North Canton, OH 44720

Stain and Odor Remover

This stain and odor remover, designed for pet owners, contains liquid enzymes that convert all organic debris from stains and odors into a liquid that can be wiped away with a cloth. This product can be used on fabrics or other surfaces and works on such substances as urine, vomit, feces, blood, and perspiration. It is nontoxic and nonflammable.

Send: $1.00 plus 50¢ postage and handling
Ask for: a pint of Nature's Miracle Stain and Odor Remover
Write to: Pets 'N People, Inc.
5312 Ironwood Street
Rancho Palos Verdes, CA 90274

For Easy Housebreaking

Cats are naturally clean animals and housebreaking them is fairly easy, but an efficient stain remover and deodorizer can make your task a real breeze. This product can be used on areas where kitty has had an accident. Simply saturate the stained area with the liquid and, after thirty seconds, blot with a paper towel. Then sponge the area with cold water and vacuum once it's dry.

Send: $1.00
Ask for: two-ounce Nilotex sample
Write to: Nilodor, Inc.
7740 Freedom Avenue, N.W.
North Canton, OH 44720

Pet Furniture

Have you been trying without success to stop your cat from scratching the fabric of some favorite armchair or climbing on the good couch? You may find the solution in this fifteen-page catalog featuring forty-one styles of feline furniture. All pieces are made from solid wood to guarantee your pet's safety. They contain no cardboard tubes or flimsy particle-board parts.

Send: $1.00 (deducted from order)
Ask for: catalog
Write to: Abeta Products, Inc.
503 Miltwood Drive, Department F
Greensboro, NC 27408

"Best of the Best" List

The Cat Fancier's Data Center is a clearinghouse of information for cat lovers. Among its many services, it reports on products used by felines and their owners. At your request, the center will send you an updated list of cat-related products that it has rated "the best of the best."

Send: a self-addressed, stamped business envelope
Ask for: "Best of the Best" list
Write to: Cat Fancier's Data Center
77 Essex Avenue
Montclair, NJ 07042

SHARING YOUR LOVE OF CATS

Color Me Purr-fect

If your children aren't treating the family cat with the love and respect he deserves, try the subtle approach—get them a special coloring book. The Animal Welfare Institute has created a cute coloring book that features charming drawings of cats living happily with families. As they color these pictures, children can't help but learn how to make your cat their best friend.

Send: 25¢
Ask for: *Kittens and Cats* coloring book
Write to: Animal Welfare Institute
P.O. Box 3650
Washington, DC 20007

Coloring Book

This free sixteen-page coloring book is designed to teach children how to protect and care for pets. The drawings, which feature kittens and cats and other animals in everyday situations, include captions that encourage children to be responsible friends to all pets.

Send: a post card
Ask for: coloring book
Write to: National Cat Protection Society
1528 West 17th Street
Long Beach, CA 90813

Living with Animals

Living with Animals is a book for young readers that depicts people and animals living together and discusses the benefits, problems, and responsibilities of human-animal relationships. It does this by examining the roles of animals in the fictional town of Critterton. By reading this book, children can learn about the basic interdependency and cooperative nature of community living. This thirty-two-page book is illustrated and offers a list of activities and further reading.

Send: $1.00
Ask for: *Living with Animals*
Write to: Massachusetts Society for the
Prevention of Cruelty to Animals
Publication Department
350 South Huntington Avenue
Boston, MA 02130
Attention: Elizabeth Stevens

Coloring Poster

Here's an activity that will not only entertain your children for hours on end but will also teach them to love domestic animals. This 22½-by-15½-inch coloring poster, based on the book *Living with Animals*, depicts a day in the life of a small town, stressing the importance of the role of animals in a community. It pictures kitty lounging comfortably on the porch, next to Grandma.

Send: $1.00
Ask for: *Living with Animals* coloring poster
Write to: Massachusetts Society for the
       Prevention of Cruelty to Animals
       Publication Department
       350 South Huntington Avenue
       Boston, MA 02130
       Attention: Elizabeth Stevens

Tenant Guidelines

Studies prove that cats and other small pets help ease the pain of loneliness, especially for senior citizens and the handicapped. Unfortunately, many elderly and disabled people mistakenly assume they can't own a cat or other pet because they are tenants. However, a 1983 federal law protects the rights of senior citizens and handicapped people who live in federally assisted rental housing to own pets. The Pet Food Institute offers a pamphlet entitled "Housing Happy Pets and Happy People," which explains the law and the responsibilities of pet-owning tenants and their landlords.

Send: a self-addressed, stamped business envelope
Ask for: tenant guidelines
Write to: Pet Food Institute
       1101 Connecticut Avenue, N.W.
       Washington, D.C. 20036

Ready for a New Kitty?

When is a child ready for the responsibility of owning and caring for a kitten? This pamphlet can help provide the answer. It lists the basic considerations a young person should take into account before getting a kitten and asks such questions as: Can you accept the fact that it won't be a baby forever? Are you prepared to give it lifetime care? Have you the time to feed, exercise, and groom it? Can you give it daily care and companionship?

Send: a self-addressed, stamped business envelope
Ask for: *So You Think You Want a Pet*
Write to: Friends of Animals, Inc.
1 Pine Street
Neptune, NJ 07753

Keeping a New Cat Happy and Healthy

Cats will be loving and charming only if they are treated the way they should be treated. Of course, *you* already know that. But it might be a good idea to convey the message to those friends who are planning to make a cat part of their family. This bulletin, which is written in both English and Spanish, explains the cat owner's basic responsibilities to his pet.

Send: a postcard
Ask for: *Thinking of Adopting a Cat?*
Write to: American Society for the
Prevention of Cruelty to Animals
441 East 92nd Street
New York, NY 10128

Kitty's First Days

If someone you know is acquiring a kitten, be sure he gets off to a good start with his new owner with this pamphlet. It is loaded with tips on how to prepare for the kitty's arrival and how to make the young feline feel comfortable in his new home. Also included are suggestions on early training, proper nutrition, and simple grooming.

Send: a self-addressed, stamped business envelope
Ask for: *Care and Feeding of Your Cat*
Write to: Carnation Company
Pet Care Center
P.O. Box 220, Department F
Pico Rivera, CA 90665

STICKERS

Colorful Cat Stamps

Add color to all your correspondence with these decorative, glossy cat stamps. Each sheet of forty full-color 1½-by-2-inch stamps features photos of cats in captivating poses with slogans such as "Cats make loving companions" and "A loved cat is a happy cat."

Send: $1.00
Ask for: cat stamps
Write to: Pet Pride
P.O. Box 1055
Pacific Palisades, CA 90272

Feline Poses

Give a distinctive touch to your notes and letters while expressing your love for cats with these stylish black-and-white cat stickers. Each set contains eight 1¼-by-2-inch stickers featuring beautifully drawn felines. The stickers show several breeds in various poses, such as sitting next to a watering can, lounging in a garden, and playing with a ball of yarn.

Send: $1.00
Ask for: set of black-and-white cat stickers
Write to: Art Studio Workshops
Department 21
518 Schilling Circle N.W.
Forest Lake, MN 55025

Colorful Cat

A picture can speak louder than words, and this colorful kitty sticker certainly says it all. A bright red, orange, and yellow cat with green eyes lounges comfortably on two rows of green and purple hearts. The sticker, about 2 inches in diameter, fits almost anywhere, from notebooks to refrigerator doors.

Send: 25¢ plus 50¢ postage and handling
Ask for: cat sticker
Write to: A.M. Associates, Inc.
212 Mass Avenue
Arlington, MA 02174

Window Decal

Any glass surface, either in your home, car, or office, will do very nicely as a showcase for the Good Luck Rainbow Cat. This transparent window decal features a happy pussy perched on a green, blue, and purple rainbow and is about 2 inches in diameter.

Send: 39¢ plus 50¢ postage and handling
Ask for: Good Luck Rainbow Cat window decal
Write to: A.M. Associates, Inc.
212 Mass Avenue
Arlington, MA 02174

Snicker Stickers

One of the best ways to express your fondness for felines is with colorful stickers. These indoor-outdoor vinyl press-on stickers measure 4½ by 3½ inches and come individually packaged in handsome polybags. Simply peel and stick on windows, doors, appliances, or notebooks. The "watchcats" design, sporting brown lettering on tan vinyl, reads, "Protective Society of Attack Cats. 24 Hour Watchcat Service." The cat family design, featuring black lettering on an aqua background, reads, "Love is all we need. United we purr. Purr-Pet-Ual devotion."

Send: $1.00 for each sticker plus a self-addressed, stamped business envelope
Ask for: "Love is all we need" or "Protective Society of Attack Cats" Snicker Stickers
Write to: Studio of Carol Lebeaux
15 Monadnock Drive
Shrewsbury, MA 01545

Sticker Sheet

By making contact with Cat Collectors—the international club whose members collect all kinds of cat-theme items—you can receive a sheet of fifteen stickers. Each sticker features a black-and-white photo of an Egyptian with the words, "Cat Collectors" underneath. The stickers are round and measure about 1 inch in diameter. Simply mention that you read about Cat Collectors in *Freebies for Cat Lovers*.

Send: a self-addressed, stamped business envelope
Ask for: set of fifteen Cat Collectors stickers and club information
Write to: Cat Collectors
31311 Blair Drive
Warren, MI 48092

Where Is Your Cat?

Many cats are needlessly put out at night to roam. Unfortunately, they must protect themselves from speeding cars on the streets and from other animals looking for a fight. You can express your concern over this practice and help influence others to keep their cats at home by displaying a bumper sticker that reads, "It's 10 P.M.—Do You Know Where Your Cat Is?"

Send: $1.00 plus 65¢ postage and handling
Ask for: "Where Is Your Cat?" bumper sticker
Write to: Tru-Beauty Distributors
760 East Park Lane
Columbia, MO 65201

Cats Are Purr-Fect

You already know that cats are perfect, as do millions of other cat lovers across the country. However, some people still need to be convinced, so display your "Cats Are Purr-Fect" bumper sticker and hammer the point home!

Send: $1.00
Ask for: "Cats Are Purr-Fect" bumper sticker
Write to: Clarke's Purr-Fect Cattery
           29 Oakwood Drive
           Oklahoma City, OK 73121

Cats Are Packed with Extra Joy

You have always loved cats, but until you brought one home you were unaware of the rewards of owning and caring for them. You have developed a deep friendship that has added a new dimension to your life. Now you can tell others about it with this bumper sticker, which reads, "Cats Are Packed with Extra Joy."

Send: $1.00
Ask for: "Cats Are Packed with Extra Joy" bumper sticker
Write to: Clarke's Purr-Fect Cattery
           29 Oakwood Drive
           Oklahoma City, OK 73121

Share Your ♥ with a Cat

The deep bond of companionship you have established with your cat makes you feel good about yourself and the world. This bumper sticker, which reads, "Share Your ♥ with a Cat," is a useful reminder of the joys of owning a cat.

Send: $1.00
Ask for: "Share Your ♥ with a Cat" bumper sticker
Write to: Clarke's Purr-Fect Cattery
29 Oakwood Drive
Oklahoma City, OK 73121

Animals Are Kind to Dumb People

Want to trigger a chuckle and still get across the message that pets are this planet's sweetest creatures? Then slap on your car this 4-by-15-inch blue and white bumper sticker that reads, "Animals Are Kind to Dumb People."

Send: $1.00 plus 65¢ postage and handling
Ask for: "Animals Are Kind to Dumb People" bumper sticker
Write to: Tru-Beauty Distributors
760 East Park Lane
Columbia, MO 65201

The More I Know Men, The More I Like My Cat

All you women cat lovers will probably enjoy showing off this hilarious red, white, and blue 4-by-15-inch bumper sticker that declares, "The More I Know Men, The More I Like My Cat." But turnabout is fair play. There's also a bumper sticker for the men that says, "The More I Know Women, The More I Like My Cat." And for those who would rather have feline companionship than human friendship, there's this message: "The More I Know People, The More I Like My Pets."

Send: $1.00 plus 65¢ postage and handling
Ask for: "The More I Know..." bumper sticker (specify men, women, or people)
Write to: Tru-Beauty Distributors
760 East Park Lane
Columbia, MO 65201

Neuter/Spay—Don't Let 'Em Stray

Help stamp out the problem of unwanted stray cats that wander the streets trying to survive. With this bumper sticker, which says, "Neuter/Spay—Don't Let 'Em Stray," you will remind others that the sensible answer to unwanted cats is neutering or spaying.

Send: $1.00
Ask for: neuter/spay bumper sticker
Write to: Friends of Animals, Inc.
1 Pine Street
Neptune, NJ 07753

I ♥ Cats

Here's an effective way you and other cat lovers can express your affection for felines. This cute bumper sticker, proclaiming "I ♥ Cats," gets the message across clearly where everyone can see it.

Send: $1.00
Ask for: "I ♥ Cats" bumper sticker
Write to: Clarke's Purr-Fect Cattery
29 Oakwood Drive
Oklahoma City, OK 73121

Cats Make Better L♥vers

If you are a cat lover with a flair for wit, then this bumper sticker should be on display on some surface in your home or car. It reads, "Cats Make Better L♥vers."

Send: $1.00
Ask for: "Cats Make Better L♥vers" bumper sticker
Write to: Clarke's Purr-Fect Cattery
29 Oakwood Drive
Oklahoma City, OK 73121

Cats Are for Huggin'

You have often indulged in the irresistible impulse to squeeze some adorable cat. Now you can encourage others to follow your example by displaying this bumper sticker, which states, "Cats Are for Huggin'."

Send: $1.00
Ask for: "Cats Are for Huggin'" bumper sticker
Write to: Clarke's Purr-Fect Cattery
29 Oakwood Drive
Oklahoma City, OK 73121

Have You Hugged Your Cat Today?

This vinyl bumper sticker with pressure-sensitive adhesive is weather-proof, measures 4 by 5 inches, and has a life expectancy of at least ten years. Now you can get this sturdy bumper sticker asking, "Have You Hugged Your Cat Today?"

Send: $1.00 plus 65¢ postage and handling
Ask for: "Have You Hugged Your Cat Today?" bumper sticker
Write to: Tru-Beauty Distributors
760 East Park Lane
Columbia, MO 65201

L♥ve Is a Sp♠yed Pet

Placing one of these beautifully designed stickers on the envelope of a friendly letter or greeting will remind not only the receiver, but everyone who handles this piece of mail, of your feelings for the well-being of millions of pets.

Send: $1.00
Ask for: five sheets of stickers
Write to: Friends of Animals
1 Pine Street
Neptune, NJ 07753

♥ Your Pets, Have Them ♠

While driving around town, why not help spread the word that you believe a loved pet should be spayed? This bright bumper sticker will provide food for thought and is sure to catch the eye of the driver behind you.

Send: $1.00
Ask for: " ♥ Your Pets, Have Them ♠ " bumper sticker
Write to: Friends of Animals, Inc.
1 Pine Street
Neptune, NJ 07753

The "Purrfect" Bumper Sticker

If you love cats and think they are the most wonderful animals in the world, let everyone know it with this bright orange bumper sticker that declares, "All Cats Are Beautiful and Purrfect."

Send: $1.00
Ask for: "Purrfect" bumper sticker
Write to: Pet Pride
P.O. Box 1055
Pacific Palisades, CA 90272

GIFTS, STATIONERY, AND NOVELTIES

Postage Stamps

Cats are pictured on postage stamps in many nations of the world. Among them, Mongolia, Saudi Arabia, Czechoslovakia, Hungary, and Equatorial Guinea have honored their favorite feline breeds by issuing series of colorful stamps. Get a packet of fifty of these original, exotic stamps.

Send: $1.00 plus 25¢ postage and handling
Ask for: cat stamps packet
Write to: Cat Stamps
P.O. Box 466
Port Washington, NY 11050

Gold-Framed Cat Stamp

Philatelic cat lovers and friends of felines are sure to admire a genuine postage stamp of a cat set in a darling miniature gold frame. Cats, Cats & More Cats has collected cat-theme postage stamps from all over the world and placed each one in a 2½-inch-square frame.

Send: $1.00 plus 50¢ postage
Ask for: gold-framed stamp
Write to: Cats, Cats & More Cats
P.O. Box 270 FF
Monroe, NY 10950

Kitty Christmas Stocking

Doesn't your pussy deserve a cute knitted Christmas stocking? With this pattern, you can knit him one in the shape of a cat paw and hang it along with the rest of the family's stockings over the fireplace so Santa can fill it with treats and toys. The pattern comes with decorating suggestions to help you personalize your kitty's stocking.

Send: $1.00 plus a 22¢ stamp
Ask for: Kitty Christmas Stocking pattern
Write to: Raveled Yarns
P.O. Box 1953
South Bend, IN 46634–1953

Cat Buttons

Are you a cat lover who can't hide your feelings? One of the most fun ways to express your love is with a colorful button. Bella Buttons has created five delightful, colorful buttons that you can wear as badges of feline honor. Each button measures 2¼ inches in diameter, has its own design, and features a different cat with one of the following sayings: "Have you hugged your cat today?" "Love me, love my cat," "Cat lover," "Pets need T.L.C." and "I love animals."

Send: $1.00 plus 22¢ stamp for each button
Ask for: cat button (specify which one)
Write to: Bella Buttons
P.O. Box 1953
South Bend, IN 46634–1953

Felt Bookmark

This unusual felt bookmark measuring 7 by 4 inches has been created for the delight of all cat lovers. In the shape of a cat's face, it is white with red ears and has green plastic eyes and a neck trimmed with red and white lace.

Send: $1.00
Ask for: cat bookmark
Write to: Satra's Purr Palace
Route 1, Box 21
Whitewater, WI 53190

Kitty Postcard

Kathy Chochrun of The Humane Society of New York has perfectly captured the charm of three adorable kittens in a basket in this photograph. Send for your black-and-white, 6-by-4-inch postcard, and use it to send messages to friends and other cat lovers.

Send: 25¢
Ask for: kitty postcard
Write to: The Humane Society of New York
306 East 59th Street
New York, NY 10022

Tabby Notepaper Tablet

If you want to dash off a quick note, what better stationery to write on than one featuring a cat? This fifty-page tablet of 8½-by-5½-inch sturdy gray paper features a black border with a tabby in the lower left corner.

Send: $1.00
Ask for: cat tablet
Write to: Cats of Class
1321 Shawnee Drive
Yellow Springs, OH 45387

Have a Purr-Fect Day!

It's a wonderful day. You feel great and want the world to know it. What better idea than to pin on your blouse or coat a button wishing everybody a purr-fect day? The button is 2 inches in diameter. It shows a smiling gray cat with turquoise eyes against a black background, and above it the words, "Have a Purr-Fect Day!"

Send: 50¢
Ask for: "Have a Purr-Fect Day!" button
Write to: The Humane Society of New York
306 East 59th Street
New York, NY 10022

Cat Bookmark

This ingenious cat bookmark makes a great gift for cat lovers since it serves a dual purpose. It not only helps you find the page you are looking for in your book but also gives you tips on feeding. The front of the bookmark features a photograph of an adorable kitty perched on a branch, and the back relays nutritional information.

Send: 25¢ plus a self-addressed, stamped business envelope
Ask for: cat bookmark
Write to: The American Humane Association
P.O. Box 1266
Denver, CO 80201

Print Pads

Do you have your cat's stamp of approval? You can show everyone you do by using a unique rubber stamp of a cat's pawprint. With this 1-inch-square print pad, you can decorate letters and envelopes, customize wrapping paper, and even jazz up your T-shirts. If you're in a really crazy mood, you can stamp yourself with the pawprint and then tell your friends that your cat walks all over you!

Send: $1.00 plus 40¢ postage and handling
Ask for: pawprint rubber stamp
Write to: Print Pads
P.O. Box 343
East Ely, NV 89315

Crochet a Cat

Turn your idle moments into crocheted gifts for your fellow cat lovers. With this easy-to-follow pattern, you can use up scraps of yarn to make an adorable 3-inch kitten that makes a great gift for your feline (and other) friends.

Send: 50¢ plus a self-addressed, stamped business envelope
Ask for: cat crochet pattern
Write to: Crocheting Forever
Mary Barbee
1134 BJ Street
Mishawaka, IN 46545

Cat Pin

Put a touch of color on jackets or blouses with this delightful piece of jewelry. The pin is about 1 inch in diameter and shows, against a white background, a smiling red, orange, and yellow cat resting on a green, blue, and violet rainbow.

Send: 40¢ plus 50¢ postage and handling
Ask for: cat pin
Write to: A.M. Associates, Inc.
212 Mass Avenue
Arlington, MA 02174

Cat Pencil

You can turn your writing instrument into visible proof of your fondness for felines with a cat pencil. This rubber-tipped pencil sports adorable orange cats, wearing red top hats and red bow ties, set against a white background.

Send: 35¢ plus 50¢ postage and handling
Ask for: cat pencil
Write to: A.M. Associates, Inc.
212 Mass Avenue
Arlington, MA 02174

Cat Pen

Make some cat lover's day by giving this pen as a gift. Complete with plastic cover to prevent mess, this ball-point pen is decorated with yellow cats wearing white top hats and white bow ties.

Send: 75¢ plus 50¢ postage and handling
Ask for: cat ball-point pen
Write to: A.M. Associates, Inc.
212 Mass Avenue
Arlington, MA 02174

Cat Puzzle

This kitty jigsaw puzzle may be the perfect way to fight boredom while waiting at the vet's office. The twenty-four-piece puzzle, made of cardboard, is a compact 7½ by 5 inches when put together. The picture on the puzzle is simple and cheerful: a plump orange kitty stretched on a row of red hearts against a white background.

Send: $1.00 plus 50¢ postage and handling
Ask for: cat puzzle
Write to: A.M. Associates, Inc.
212 Mass Avenue
Arlington, MA 02174

Mimi Vang Olsen Notecard

Glowing colors and beguiling expressions bring to life the cats in this beautiful series of notecards designed especially for the Humane Society of New York by noted pet portrait painter Mimi Vang Olsen. The series includes two 5-by-7-inch postcards, one featuring a curled-up gray cat and the other an adorable feline family. You can also obtain any of three fold-over cards with envelopes: two cats and a beagle; a cat and a mutt; or a black and white kitten on his back next to a friendly dog.

Send: $1.00 per card
Ask for: Mimi Vang Olsen notecard (specify choice)
Write to: The Humane Society of New York
306 East 59th Street
New York, NY 10022

Cat Gift Tag

Add a feline touch to your gift giving by attaching a cat-theme gift tag to your present. The 1¾-by-6-inch tag features a yarn tassle and a full-color print of a cute kitten. As an added feature, the cat tag doubles as a bookmark.

Send: $1.00
Ask for: gift tag
Write to: The Chatco Collection
P.O. Box 59
Batesville, IN 47006

Purr-fect Care Bookmark

This free 8-inch-long cat-theme bookmark offered by the Animal Protection Institute of America is unique. First, it offers tips on the care of your cat. Second, it is designed so that the head of a kitten and his paws will always stick out at the top edge of the page you are marking.

Send: a self-addressed, stamped business envelope
Ask for: Purr-fect Care of Cats bookmark
Write to: Animal Protection Institute of America
P.O. Box 22505
Sacramento, CA 95822

CAT RIGHTS AND WELFARE

Eliminating Pound Seizure

Pound seizure is the practice of requisitioning unclaimed animals from public pounds and shelters for experimentation purposes. This means that the helpless kitty you picked up off the street and took to a shelter, thinking you saved it from death, may be given to a laboratory. You have a right to know that an animal is going to be safe in a shelter, and pound seizure takes away this right. This guide, advocating the elimination of pound seizure, uncovers the inadequacies of the Animal Welfare Act and offers suggestions for organizing an anti-pound-seizure campaign.

Send: a postcard
Ask for: *A Guide for Eliminating Pound Seizure*
Write to: The American Anti-Vivisection Society
Suite 204, Noble Plaza
801 Old York Road
Jenkintown, PA 19046–1685

The Animal Welfare Act

The federal Animal Welfare Act, first passed by Congress in 1966, stipulates humane care, treatment, and transportation for pets and other animals. This pamphlet provides details about the law and its history, as well as the requirements that constitute humane care and treatment of cats and dogs. These include housing, handling, feeding, watering, sanitation, ventilation, transportation, and protection against extremes of hot and cold weather. There is also a section on breeders, who must be licensed and inspected periodically, and one on traveling with your pet. Protection for stray and stolen pets, as well as pets used for research, are also discussed.

Send: a postcard
Ask for: *The Animal Welfare Act: How It Protects Your Dog and Cat*
Write to: APHIS Publications Distribution
G186 Federal Building
Hyattsville, MD 20782

The Vicious Cycle

This bulletin illustrates, with poignant drawings, the ordeals unwanted kittens go through—sleeping in dirty alleys, becoming filthy and diseased, and suffering hunger and abuse—and then explains the benefits of neutering and spaying. It also outlines the neutering program created by Friends of Animals, Inc., a nonprofit organization devoted to the welfare of animals.

Send: a self-addressed, stamped business envelope
Ask for: *The Vicious Cycle*
Write to: Friends of Animals, Inc.
1 Pine Street
Neptune, NJ 07753

Morris Animal Foundation

There are scores of societies and foundations all over the country devoted to the welfare of animals. Among them is the Morris Animal Foundation, a nonprofit charitable organization. This pamphlet tells you about the goals and structure of this institution, as well as its achievements in the field of veterinary medicine. Among other things, the foundation developed nutritional requirements for cats and discovered interferon, a protein substance generated by the body that slows the growth of some viruses and may be helpful in fighting diseases like feline leukemia.

Send: a postcard
Ask for: *Keep Your Interest in Animals Alive Forever*
Write to: Morris Animal Foundation
45 Inverness Drive East
Englewood, CO 80112

American Humane Association Publications List

The American Humane Association, which has been in existence for over one hundred years, strives to prevent cruelty to animals and fosters the well-being of pets across the nation. Part of its effort includes the publication of the educational literature described in this list. It provides detailed explanations of the pamphlets and teaching booklets available from the association and also offers information on posters, bookmarks, and films.

Send: a self-addressed, stamped business envelope
Ask for: free list of educational materials
Write to: The American Humane Association
P.O. Box 1266
Denver, CO 80201

Surplus Dogs and Cats

Cats are about thirty to forty-five times more prolific than humans, but only a small percentage of the felines born daily are destined to complete their life span with a caring owner. There are not enough responsible pet owners to provide homes, and unwanted pets are either put to death in shelters or left to starve, be shot, poisoned, or run over. This brochure details the steps you can take to fight pet overpopulation and gives the latest statistics on the problem.

Send: 50¢ plus a self-addressed, stamped business envelope
Ask for: "Pet Overpopulation"
Write to: The American Humane Association
P.O. Box 1266
Denver, CO 80201

Pet Owners Beware

Theft of pets is a nationwide problem in our country. Cats, even licensed or registered ones, are frequently stolen from unwary owners by unscrupulous dealers and sold to research laboratories that use animals in experiments. This brochure will open your eyes and alert you to the fact that your feline companion could easily become the victim of vivisection, part of a medical industry supported by vast public and private funds.

Send: a postcard
Ask for: *Pet Owners Beware*
Write to: The American Anti-Vivisection Society
Suite 204, Noble Plaza
801 Old York Road
Jenkintown, PA 19046–1685

Opposing Vivisection

This twenty-page booklet describes the efforts of caring Americans who seek to halt the horrible destruction of millions of animals that are used for experimentation. The booklet offers suggestions on how you can help stop this heinous practice.

Send: a postcard
Ask for: *Why We Oppose Vivisection*
Write to: The American Anti-Vivisection Society
Suite 204, Noble Plaza
801 Old York Road
Jenkintown, PA 19046–1685

Experiments with Living Animals

In the name of science, vivisectionists have for years performed horrible experiments on animals, causing needless pain and suffering to defenseless creatures. This startling forty-six-page booklet reveals many shocking examples of how an $800-million-a-year industry uses and abuses millions of animals in the laboratory. Unfortunately, according to the National Academy of Sciences, 55,000 felines a year are among the victims of the vivisection mills. Citing case histories and dramatic statistics, this booklet presents a strong argument for the abolition of vivisection—a goal it says can be accomplished only by the concerted efforts of an informed and aroused public.

Send: a postcard
Ask for: *The Case Book of Experiments with Living Animals*
Write to: The American Anti-Vivisection Society
Suite 204, Noble Plaza
801 Old York Road
Jenkintown, PA 19046–1685

PUBLICATIONS AND ORGANIZATIONS

Cats Magazine

Now in its forty-second year, *Cats Magazine* offers articles, photographs, poems, and cartoons about cats in a slick and colorful format. Its columns on the care and health of cats, articles on breeding and showing, news of cats worldwide, and letters from readers make for fascinating reading.

Send: $1.00
Ask for: sample issue of *Cats Magazine*
Write to: Cats Magazine
P.O. Box 290037
Port Orange, FL 32029

Feline and Canine Times

This newsletter is published by Feline and Canine Friends, Inc., a nonprofit California corporation devoted to animal welfare. It features articles about animals, medical advice for pets, tips on pet care, and information about shelters and spaying programs.

Send: a self-addressed, stamped business envelope
Ask for: sample issue of *Feline and Canine Times*
Write to: Feline and Canine Friends, Inc.
505 North Bush Street
Anaheim, CA 92805

Time for Animals

Time for Animals is a periodical put out by the Los Angeles Society for the Prevention of Cruelty to Animals. The tabloid-size publication contains book reviews, updates on legislation for the protection of animals, letters from readers, poems, news on animal art shows, and information about the treatment of animals in film, among other things.

Send: a postcard
Ask for: issue of *Time for Animals*
Write to: Los Angeles Society for the Prevention of Cruelty to
Animals
5026 West Jefferson Boulevard
Los Angeles, CA 90016

Pet News

Advances in veterinary medicine, book reviews, information about adoption, and tips about how to care for your cat are some of the subjects covered by this readable newsletter published by the Humane Society of New York. Profiles of the society's animals are also featured —including stories that introduce you to some very special cats. Each newsletter is illustrated with drawings and photographs.

Send: 25¢ postage and handling
Ask for: issue of *The Humane Society of New York News*
Write to: The Humane Society of New York
306 East 59th Street
New York, NY 10022

Animals' Agenda

As a cat owner concerned about the rights of your feline, you should also be concerned about animal rights in general. This monthly, forty-eight page news magazine deals with our relationship with animals and how it can be improved. Thirty-five contributing editors from all over the United States bring you news, opinions, articles, profiles, interviews, and reviews pertaining to animal rights and welfare. Remember, your kitten is a part of the larger animal kingdom!

Send: a postcard
Ask for: free sample copy of *Animals' Agenda*
Write to: The Animals' Agenda
P.O. Box 5234
Westport, CT 06881

The Mewspaper

The Mewspaper is the cat's meow. Kids who love felines will have fun reading their own newsletter that's all about cats. The pages are filled with educational and entertaining features, including charming illustrations, games, puzzles, contests, and stories about the lore and history of cats.

Send: $1.00
Ask for: sample copy of *The Mewspaper*
Write to: The Mewspaper Publishing Company
P.O. Box 1240, Department FCL
Madison Square Station
New York, NY 10159

Pen Pals for Pet Lovers

The World Wide Pet Lovers' Society was established in 1984 to bring pet lovers from around the globe together by means of a pen-pal exchange. It now has more than 6,000 members who correspond with each other. Matchups are arranged by age and pet interest of each applicant. You can obtain information on how to join.

Send: name, address, age, pet interest, and $1.00 plus a self-addressed, stamped business envelope
Ask for: Pet Pen Pal Service
Write to: WWPLS
Department CL
P.O. Box 9585
Beaumont, TX 77709

Cat Mews Newsletter

This bimonthly newsletter is aimed at cat owners who want to maintain their cats' health and happiness. It features in-depth articles on how to prevent health problems before they get started. A free gift will be sent to you with your subscription if you mention *Freebies for Cat Lovers*.

Send: 25¢
Ask for: sample issue of *Cat Mews Newsletter*
Write to: Cat Mews Publication
Suite 218
230 Hilton Avenue
Hempstead, NY 11550

Delta Society

This nonprofit, public service organization is dedicated to furthering the beneficial contacts between people and animals. It's astonishing what contact with an animal can do for a person's emotional and physical health. For example, simply watching a cat play can lower your stress level and blood pressure. The Delta Society promotes scientific research in human-animal interaction and helps people start local pet therapy programs.

Send: a self-addressed, stamped business envelope
Ask for: information packet
Write to: The Delta Society
P.O. Box 1080
Renton, WA 98057

Cat Fanciers Membership Packet

Did you ever stop to consider how much more there is to owning a cat than feeding and providing adequate care for it? Get a glimpse of the complex and often fascinating world of cat breeding and cat shows with the American Cat Fanciers Association membership packet. It includes information about the organization, its goals and programs, an application form for membership, a bulletin featuring reviews of shows and lists of winners, an application for registering your cat with the association, and a certificate of breeding.

Send: a postcard
Ask for: American Cat Fanciers Association membership packet
Write to: American Cat Fanciers Association
P.O. Box 203
Point Lookout, MO 65726

Somali Cat Club of America

The Somali is a long-haired Abyssinian that has become a popular new breed. This interesting brochure explains how Abyssinians got their long-hair genes, what they look like, how they behave, and many other facts about this beautiful feline. The brochure also explains how you can join other Somali clubs.

Send: $1.00
Ask for: Somali cat brochure
Write to: Somali Cat Club of America
10 Western Boulevard
Gillette, NJ 07933

Siamese News Quarterly

If Siamese cats are your favorite breed, then you will enjoy reading a sample copy of the *Siamese News Quarterly*. This publication contains articles, cartoons, and cat-care information aimed at lovers of Siamese cats.

Send: 56¢ in postage stamps
Ask for: sample issue of *Siamese News Quarterly*
Write to: Siamese Cat Society of America, Inc.
1026 East Ganley Road
Tucson, AZ 85706

Cat Collectors

Cat Collectors is an international club whose members enjoy the common interest of collecting cat figurines, books, artwork, advertisements, calendars, needlework, jewelry, and any other items pertaining to cats. The club issues a letter of information that details the goals of the organization and describes its bimonthly newsletter. There is also information about how you can become a member and receive a sheet of fifteen cat stickers.

Send: a self-addressed, stamped business envelope
Ask for: Cat Collectors letter of information
Write to: Cat Collectors
31311 Blair Drive
Warren, MI 48092

Voice of the Voiceless

This is a bimonthly magazine dedicated to speaking out on the welfare of animals. Attractively illustrated, this publication brings to its concerned readers stories, poems, and up-to-date information about the rights—and abuses—of animals.

    Send: a postcard
  Ask for: sample issue of *Voice of the Voiceless*
Write to: Voice of the Voiceless
              P.O. Box 17403
              Foy Station
              Los Angeles, CA 90017

Shelter News

This quarterly newsletter gives you up-to-date information on the latest laws that affect the welfare of cats. It also seeks the cooperation of readers in ridding the streets, highways, and alleyways of abandoned or stray small animals.

    Send: a postcard
  Ask for: sample issue of *Shelter News*
Write to: National Cat Protection Society
              P.O. Box 6218
              Long Beach, CA 90806

CATALOGS

The Hairy Beast

The Hairy Beast offers notecards and stationery adorned with beautiful drawings of cats. In addition, its new catalog features an extensive array of stained-glass lampshades and clocks depicting various breeds of cats.

Send: $1.00
Ask for: cat catalog
Write to: The Hairy Beast
Route 1, Box 334
Hedgesville, WV 25427

Satra's Purr Palace

Satra's Purr Palace has been in the cat business since 1956 and offers all kinds of items for cats and cat lovers, including toys, pencils, recipes for kitty cookies, stationery, and gift boxes. The catalog is printed twice a year, once in the spring and once in the fall.

Send: $1.00
Ask for: Satra's Purr Palace catalog
Write to: Satra's Purr Palace
Route 1, Box 21
Whitewater, WI 53190

Wild Cats

This cat-theme firm carries high-quality gifts for cat lovers. Two catalogs, one of them in color, offer an exceptional variety of T-shirts, jewelry, figurines, notecards, prints, tote bags, rubber stamps, teapots, and more.

Send: $1.00
Ask for: Wild Cats gift catalogs
Write to: Wild Cats, Inc.
Rainbow Market
40 North Market Street
Charleston, SC 29401

Du-Say's

Du-Say's, which has been serving pets and their owners for more than fifty years, has a forty-two-page color catalog of products for cats and dogs. Among the items it offers are a refrigerated automatic feeder, an electronic flea collar, designer fragrances, and even a miniature circus tent for pussy to nap in.

Send: a postcard
Ask for: catalog
Write to: Du-Say's
215 Seventh Street
Picayune, MS 39466

Blythe Designs

Blythe Designs has come up with a special collection of hand-crafted treasures for cat lovers, cats, and their friends. This free catalog features cuddly one-of-a-kind stuffed cats and cat-theme items from pot-holders to baby bibs.

Send: a self-addressed, stamped business envelope
Ask for: catalog
Write to: Blythe Designs
P. O. Box 17506
Seattle, WA 98107

Felix

For the health and happiness of your cat, and for your pleasure and enjoyment, this cat lovers' catalog brings you a collection of forty high-quality cat products, many of them manufactured by Felix. Toys include a yarn octopus and a crochet ball, and there are also scratching boards and climbing posts, books on cats, and grooming products like foam shampoo and Katnix, a crystalline powder that repels cats and keeps them away from rugs and furniture. Felix has been in the cat business for more than thirty years.

Send: a postcard
Ask for: Felix catalog
Write to: Felix
3623 Fremont Avenue, N.
Seattle, WA 98103

Cat-Theme Sportswear

The Paws and Claws designer sportswear line features soft fleece suits, with different breeds of cats silkscreened on the tops, in navy, red, white, gray, jade, pink, and plum, for adults and teenagers. A pawprint design on a pant leg or sleeve is optional. This brochure gives complete information about colors and sizes for crew-neck sweatshirts, sweatshirt vests, fleece suits, and long-sleeve T-shirts.

Send: a postcard
Ask for: Paws and Claws designer originals brochure
Write to: Famous Fido's, Inc.
1527 West Devon
Chicago, IL 60660

Dr. Daniels

For more than 100 years Dr. Daniels has been offering a complete line of pharmaceutical products for cats, including skin salve, ear-cleaning solution, tapeworm medicine, and catnip bags. Liniment for strains and muscular aches, nontoxic deodorizer tablets, and lotion for skin ailments are also offered. This catalog features illustrations and specifies the available sizes of all products.

Send: a postcard
Ask for: Dr. Daniels catalog
Write to: Dr. A. C. Daniels, Inc.
               Department CL
               Worcester Road
               Webster, MA 01570

Rubber Stamp Kitties

Don't let your love of cats go unnoticed! Decorate stationery, wrapping paper, invitations, recipe cards, bookmarks, notes, or envelopes with original rubber-stamp cats. C Note Enterprises' catalog features more than thirty cat designs to tickle your imagination. An order for the catalog will also get you a coupon worth $1.00 off your first purchase.

Send: $1.00
Ask for: C Note Enterprises catalog
Write to: C Note Enterprises
               2325 Pennland Drive
               Sacramento, CA 95825

Chatco

Chatco—which means "cat company," from the French word *chat* for cat—offers the cat lover an interesting collection of items, such as cat-theme quilts and rugs, that are fun, unusual, and practical. Its catalog is designed to help you find that special gift for a friend or useful item for yourself. Founded on a love of cats and a kinship with others who cherish them, Chatco donates a percentage of its net profits to cat-protection shelters and agencies.

Send: $1.00
Ask for: The Chatco Collection catalog
Write to: Chatco
P.O. Box 59
Batesville, IN 47006

The Cat's Whiskers

The Cat's Whiskers is a firm that offers a wide variety of gifts and toys for the cat and the cat lover. The collection features a black-and-white kitten pitcher, a kitten treasure box, a kitten planter, a cat T-shirt, and a cat Christmas sock, among other items.

Send: a postcard
Ask for: The Cat's Whiskers catalog
Write to: The Cat's Whiskers
1104 N.W. 30th
Oklahoma City, OK 73118

Pedigrees

Pedigrees' pet catalog is a colorful forty-page guide to shopping at home for delightful gifts for you and your cat-lover friends. There is everything from a cat-crossing sign for the front yard to designer cat beds color-coordinated with your decor at home.

Send: a postcard
Ask for: the pet catalog
Write to: Pedigrees
P.O. Box 110, PB87
Spencerport, NY 14559

Cat Tales

Cat Tales specializes in cat stickers and rubber stamps. Its catalog features realistic and stylized cats, pawprint rubber stamps, and Kitty Cucumber seals. Accompanying the catalog are samples of stickers and a membership application to the Cat Tales Sticker Club. The club offers special free stickers, a chance for members to trade with each other, and the latest information about new stickers on the market.

Send: a postcard
Ask for: sticker catalog
Write to: Cat Tales
1732 Birmingham Boulevard
Birmingham, MI 48009

Cat Outfitters

The Cat Outfitters catalog contains American and English hand-crafted products made by cat-loving craftspeople who pay the utmost attention to cat appeal and safety. Among the items featured in the catalog are a wicker bed, a window perch, an English grooming tool, gourmet treats, and many unusual cat toys.

Send: $1.00 (refundable with order)
Ask for: catalog
Write to: The Cat Outfitters
Catalog Department
P.O. Box 27646, Department FFCL
Albuquerque, NM 87124

Bizzaro

Kitty lovers with a flair for fun will purr with delight while leafing through this twenty-one-page catalog loaded with humorous rubber stamps. The stamps featuring cats include kissing kittens, a dancing kitten, and a tiger cat. There is also a cat-theme set, which consists of four rubber stamps packed in their own storage box. The set, a perfect gift for the cat lover, portrays a kitten, a Persian, a Siamese, and a tomcat.

Send: $1.00 (refundable with order)
Ask for: catalog
Write to: Bizzaro Rubber Stamps
P.O. Box 16160
Rumford, RI 02916

Veterinary Products

This eighty-page mail-order catalog, available to the layman, offers a comprehensive selection of products for enhancing the quality of life of your prized kitty. Furniture, feeders, and grooming aids are featured, as well as food supplements, vaccines, and flea collars. There is also a section devoted to cat books.

Send: a postcard
Ask for: Animal Veterinary Products catalog
Write to: Animal Veterinary Products, Inc.
P.O. Box 1267
Galesburg, IL 61401

The Gold Bug

This firm is exclusively devoted to selling pet-design jewelry in fourteen-karat gold, ten-karat gold, sterling silver, and gold plate. Most of the charms featured in the catalog can also be converted into stick pins, tie tacks, earrings, cuff links, or charm holders.

Send: $1.00
Ask for: The Gold Bug catalog
Write to: The Gold Bug
3464 Burnett Drive
Murrysville, PA 15668

Rawcliffe

This magnificent forty-eight-page catalog features pewter artwork by the Rawcliffe Corporation. The collection includes a series of twelve cat figurines, from 1 to 3 inches high, in various charming poses. There are also cat charms of several breeds, including the Himalayan and the American Shorthair.

Send: a self-addressed, stamped business envelope
Ask for: Rawcliffe Pet Lovers' catalog
Write to: Rawcliffe Corporation
Retail Catalog Division
155 Public Street
Providence, RI 02903

Art Studio Workshop

This twenty-page catalog presents work by award-winning artist Patricia A. McLaughlin. It includes postcards and prints, note cards and envelopes, and original greeting cards featuring several breeds of cats. Personalized Pet Adoption certificates and Best Cat Award certificates are also offered.

Send: $1.00
Ask for: catalog
Write to: Art Studio Workshop
518 Schilling Circle,
Department 21
Forest Lake, MN 55025

Cats of Class

Cats of Class offers handsome handmade cat gifts for feline lovers in a wide variety of fabrics. This catalog allows the potential buyer to choose fabrics that match his or her home decor, with items available in most colors. The selection of gifts includes cat pillows, cat napkin holders, scented cats, cat magnets, and stenciled cat designs framed on wooden hoops.

Send: $1.00
Ask for: Cats of Class Cat-a-log
Write to: Cats of Class
1321 Shawnee Drive
Yellow Springs, OH 45387

Cats, Cats & More Cats

With an alley cat named Hasenpfeffer as its honorary chairman of the board, this company specializes in offering unique, fun, cat-theme products. Among the more than 100 delightful gifts featured in its catalog are a Christmas stocking for your pussy and a kitty album to keep his photos and record his special moments.

Send: 50¢
Ask for: catalog
Write to: Cats, Cats & More Cats
P.O. Box 270-FF
Monroe, NY 10950

Animal City

Animal City, the wholesale division of Petco Animal Supplies, has a 130-page catalog of almost every item you could want for your cat, from veterinary supplies to grooming equipment to cat trees.

Send: a postcard
Ask for: Animal City catalog
Write to: Petco/Animal City
P.O. Box 269024
San Diego, CA 92126–9024

Personalized Bank Checks

The Kansas Bank Note Company, a major nationwide supplier of bank forms and a commercial check printer, offers a series of feline checks. A free brochure shows twenty-four breeds of cats that can be reproduced on checks with sporty denim, distinctive parchment, or sparkling white backgrounds. These fine custom-made checks are acceptable for use with your account at any bank. The brochure includes a price list and comes with samples of checks.

Send: a postcard
Ask for: illustrated brochure and samples of feline checks
Write to: Kansas Bank Note Company
P.O. Box 360
Fredonia, KS 66736

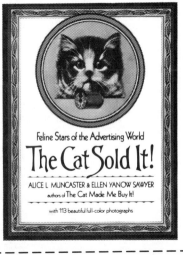